Gay Marriage,
What Does Almighty God Say?

Message from Almighty God to the Prime Minister of the United Kingdom on the Same Sex Marriage Act.

Apostle Dr Max Matonhodze

Published by Max Matonhodze

Publishing partner: Paragon Publishing, Rothersthorpe

First published 2023

© Max Matonhodze, 2023

The rights of Max Matonhodze to be identified as the author of this work have been asserted by him in accordance with the Copyright, Designs and Patents Act of 1988. All rights reserved; no part of this publication may be reproduced, stored in a retrieval system, or transmitted in any form or by any means, electronic, mechanical, photocopying, recording or otherwise without the prior written consent of the publisher or a licence permitting copying in the UK issued by the Copyright Licensing Agency Ltd. www.cla.co.uk

ISBN 978-1-78792-018-7

Book design, layout and production management by Into Print
www.intoprint.net
+44 (0)1604 832149

Dedicated to

Almighty God,
The Father of lights, with whom there is no variation
or shadow of turning.

James 1:17 NKJV

Contents

Preface: How this book came about 9

Chapter 1: The Message from God Almighty as received on the 6th January 2014 15

Summary: Carnal relationship between men on men – also known as homosexual or gay relationships – what does God Almighty say?

1.1 The greatest commandments are to love the Lord our God with all our heart, soul, strength and mind and our neighbour as ourselves 17

1.2 The authority of the word of God: heaven and earth shall pass away but the word will not pass away 18

1.3 The source of carnal feeling of men to men: what the scriptures say .. 19

1.4 The Parable of the Wheat and the Tares tells us the origin and source of carnal relationships between men and men (and all other forms of evil and rebellion against God) is satan 21

1.5 He who made them in the beginning made them male and female: the union between man and woman was decreed and instituted by God himself.. 22

1.6 The relationship between a husband and wife is a mirror image of the relationship between Christ and the Church 23

1.7 The grace of God for repentance and salvation has appeared to all – we are all invited to accept it 24

1.8 The biblical role of government is to uphold righteousness for righteousness exalts a nation, but sin is a reproach to any people. 25

1.9 The difference between civil partnership and marriage is celebration. By endorsing gay marriage, the government is upholding celebration of unrighteousness and sin, this is not love of people who are gay but deception 25

1.10 It is the duty of the church to intercede for the nation and ameliorate God's judgement. It is the duty of every true child of God to pray and intercede for the nation to ameliorate God's judgement 26

1.11 Word of caution to the child of God – let not this matter consume you and get you out of focus.. 27

1.12 Word to the gay and lesbian, God loves you and so do I, I have a special message for you at the end of which you need to make a choice 27

1.12.1 To receive His promises you need to understand how to overcome the wicked one.. 29

1.12.2 To overcome the wicked one you need to understand the nature of satan 29

1.12.3 To overcome the wicked one you need to understand the origins of satan 30

1.12.4 Understanding the believer's victory over satan 31

1.12.5 Understanding the authority of the believer to bind and rebuke satan in the name of the Lord Jesus Christ 33

1.12.6 Understanding the victory over satan through the confession of the blood of the Lord Jesus Christ. 33

1.12.7 The destiny of satan is the lake of fire for all eternity 35

Chapter 2: Author's explanatory notes: We need a standard of truth. .. 37

Chapter 3: Author's explanatory notes: We need love and compassion for gay people 39

Chapter 4: Author's explanatory notes: Why Same Sex Marriage works against gay people.. 41

Chapter 5: Author's explanatory notes: Civil partnership Act and Same Sex Marriage Act-why the latter crosses the line from heaven 43

Chapter 6: Author's explanatory notes: The role of Government in God's agenda for mankind 45

Chapter 7: Author's explanatory notes: The duty of the church to intercede for the nation and ameliorate judgement 47

Chapter 8: Author's exploratory notes: The benefits of repealing Same Sex Marriage Act 57

Chapter 9: There is a way back for the gay and lesbian 60

References 64

Chapter 10: Reflections of other Church Leaders 65

Chapter 11: Reflections of Apostle Bishop Cephas Nyemba 71

Chapter 12: Conclusion.. 73

About the Author 77

Preface

How this book came about

On the 6th of January 2014, I woke up as normal preparing to go to work. I had lived in Dudley Metropolitan Borough of the West Midlands since 1st February 1995. In every other respect it was a normal January Monday morning. Then God spoke to me – clearly: I have a message which I want you to give to the Prime Minister. What? I asked within myself – have I heard that correctly? I turned round to see if there was anybody with me. I was alone. I started praying – God is it you speaking to me? The voice came again unmistakably – "Yes it's Me – I have a message for you for the Prime Minister, write it down."

The message started coming – downloading literally. I went to work as usual as a Consultant Respiratory Physician in a busy District General Hospital in the West Midlands of the United Kingdom.

I had heard from God from time to time and on many occasions over the last three decades since I became a born-again Christian. I had learnt and understood that whenever God speaks to me, that word from God must be based, supported, and confirmed with two or three witnesses from the written word of God, the scriptures. (Deuteronomy 19:15, Matthew 18:16, 2 Corinthians 13:1, Hebrews 10:28).

I came back from work, started writing the message which Almighty God had been downloading to me all day. I could feel the presence of God and the anointing as I started putting the message down. Some of the things I was being told and shown from the scriptures were startling to me – they were new. I was told things I had not known before.

God was speaking to me about the Same Sex Marriage Act which had been enacted in November 2013. The act had crossed a line from heaven.

This message must not be construed as homophobic because it is a message of love to the Prime Minister of the United Kingdom (as well as other world leaders) and love to the gay community and to the nation of the United Kingdom and indeed every nation of Planet Earth. It answers and gives amazing clarity to questions which many people have been asking and struggling to get clarity on. It exposes the deception with which the enemy of God and mankind satan wants to entice people into bondage. It reveals who is behind same sex attraction and the way out which Almighty God has provided for every man and woman.

It is a message from the God of all mercy, God who is love, God who sent Jesus Christ to suffer and die so that every single person can be accepted by God and be given the gift of forgiveness of sin and eternal life. It is a message of eternal truth that does not change with time or fashion. Almighty God says I am God and I do not change therefore you sons of Jacob are not consumed (Malachi 3:6).

Please understand this – **Romans 3:23** tells us: **For all have sinned and fall short of the glory of God (NKJV).**

In **Isaiah 53:6** we read: **All we like sheep have gone astray; we have turned, everyone to his own way; and the Lord laid on Him (Jesus Christ) the iniquity of us all (NKJV).**

To access forgiveness of sin through Jesus Christ, one needs repentance – which is changing your mind to agree with God as to what is right and what is wrong. You come to God and say, "I was wrong all along and you are right – thank you for sending Jesus Christ to die for my sin, to shed blood so that my sin may be forgiven. I acknowledge you Jesus Christ as Lord of my life from today. I believe that God raised you from the dead and you are alive today. From today I will live my life for you. I will follow you Jesus Christ from today."

Without repentance, there is no access to forgiveness of sin which is in Jesus Christ.

That is why Jesus Christ said in **Luke 13:3** and **Luke 13:5: "I tell you, no; but unless you repent you will all likewise perish".** Repentance is not grovelling, or coming to God begging for forgiveness in desperation – it is changing your mind, and changing allegiance, from agreeing with the enemy satan to agreeing with God, from aligning with the enemy satan to aligning with God, from embracing the enemy satan and his deception to embracing the God of Jesus Christ. What follows is then embracing the word of God and allowing the word of God to transform the way you think, so that you think like God, to transform the way you speak so that you speak like God, and transform the way you act, so that you act like God.

That is why His word says in **Romans 12:1-2: I beseech you therefore, brethren, by the mercies of God, that you present your bodies a living sacrifice, holy, acceptable to God, which is your reasonable service.**

2 And do not be conformed to this world, but be transformed by the renewing of your mind, that you may prove what is that good and acceptable and perfect will of God (NKJV).

Presenting your body as a living sacrifice means setting yourself apart for God to seek His purpose and His will. This is a decision followed by a declaration: **"Lord Jesus Christ, you can have me, with all that I am and with all that I am not I give my life to you. Do what you want with me".**

You also need to declare to the enemy satan: **"You have nothing in me and I have nothing in you, I command you in the name of Jesus Christ to let me go and serve God. I know that you were defeated publicly and openly by Jesus Christ on the cross and you have a one way ticket to the lake of fire for all eternity".**

Following this you need to decide and commit to the process of embracing and studying His word under guidance of servants of God, memorising key scriptures and allowing His word to transform the way you think, the way to speak and the way you act. The word of God reveals to you the mind of God.

The message in this book explains the duty of love by all mankind to men and women who are gay, the duty not to judge prematurely and crucially, the duty to tell the truth in love.

It also crucially explains the duty of every government across the nations of Planet Earth to uphold the truth and not to deceive people to gain easy and cheap popularity. It explains what marriage is and what it is not. It explains the crucial difference between civil partnership and same sex marriage. It explains why Civil Partnership is an acknowledgement of an arrangement between two consenting adults and why the Same Sex Marriage Act of 2013 in the United Kingdom crosses the line of heaven. This act upholds deception to gay people with the potential of leading gay people to eternal judgement by God, which essentially means missing heaven and going into damnation eternally in hell.

This message from God explains the duty of love we all owe to gay men and women, and which means kindness, equal opportunity including in education, work, accommodation and giving them right to participate freely in society.

It explains further that while Civil Partnership Act acknowledges an arrangement made between two adults, marriage as ordained by Lord God Almighty, can only be between a man and a woman and the Same Sex Marriage Act of 2013 must be repealed because it is a deceptive legislation and puts the nation at risk of judgement from heaven because the word of God teaches us in Proverbs 14:34 that righteousness exalts a nation, but sin is a reproach to any people. The word reproach means an expression of rebuke and disapproval. When Almighty God rebukes and disapproves a nation that means the nation is at risk of judgement. The dimensions of the judgement that comes from Almighty God are explained in depth in *Chapter 7*.

It took me three weeks to complete writing the message. It was downloaded from the throne of grace in heaven. It was and still is a mind-blowing message.

I woke up on the morning of Monday 27th January 2014 feeling message nearly done. Before I left the house however, God spoke to me again, the message was clear: "Before the end of the day, today, this message must be in Number 10

Downing Street, with the Prime Minister". I got very concerned as at this point it was not at all clear how I was going to do this.

I reached work and as my first session was administration, I immediately called my secretary to the office whom I thought being native born could probably know a bit about how I could send a message to the Prime Minister.

I explained to her the situation and asked her the question: "How do I send a message to the Prime Minister?" "Max – I have no idea", was her reply.

I realised I was no further forward. I thought – let me go on the internet, to find more information about 10 Downing Street, the official residence of the Prime Minister of the United Kingdom.

To my surprise, I quickly found out that 10 Downing Street has a switchboard, and the telephone number was freely available on the internet. This was a great step forward. I had never known this before.

I picked up my mobile phone and called the listed number. It was readily answered. I asked the question – "how do I send a message to the Prime Minister?" The attendant who answered the phone explained I could send a message a thousand characters in length to the Prime Minister and gave me the web address.

I had made real progress. As the message was 23 pages in length, I quickly thought I would summarise the message in a thousand characters, ask the team who maintain the Planet Ministries website to upload the message to the site and I would put a link to the full message on the summarised message.

I quickly called the website team and explained, they promptly uploaded the message and sent me the link.

That evening of the 27th January 2014, I arrived home and sent the message to the Prime Minister as follows:

Dear Honourable Prime Minister,

Three weeks ago, I received a message from Almighty God for the Prime Minister of the United Kingdom. The government of the United Kingdom has done a great work in enacting laws that keep this nation safe, however the Same Sex Marriage act crosses the line from heaven and must be repealed. The full message from Almighty God can be accessed at https://planetministries.org.uk/message/gaymarriage

This message is not partisan and is not based on self-interest. The Prime Minister has total and complete liberty to ignore this message. If he does, however, He risks judgement from heaven.

I would recommend that the Prime Minister authenticates this message with reference to Her Majesty.

If you need any aspect of this message clarified please feel free to contact me on this telephone number […] and email […]

(I put my mobile telephone number and personal e-mail address).

Yours Sincerely

[…] *(my name, address, designation, telephone number, email address).*

In Chapter 1 of this book is the full message which I received from Almighty God in January 2014. The message is presented here in its original form. This message has been on the Planet Ministries website with unrestricted public access until July 2022 when the preparation of this book started. The chapters that follow are the author's further explanatory notes to help the reader gain more understanding of the critical points of this message. Chapters 10 and 11 are reflections from selected Church Leaders whom I asked to preview the draft manuscript and have their own independent reflections on the contents of this book pre-publication.

You will notice that reference to satan is put with a small letter s – this is my way of reminding every reader that satan was defeated publicly and openly by Jesus Christ on the cross when He died and rose again and that when one acknowledges Jesus Christ as Lord and believes that God raised Him from the dead, not only are you saved and forgiven, but you are also given victory over satan in the name of Jesus Christ. You are given authority to command satan to cease operating in the affairs of your life in the name of Jesus Christ. This is explained in more depth in the book Vessels of Excellence by the same author. Please also note that all quotations from the bible are from the New King James Version, unless otherwise stated.

Please note that in Chapter 10, *Reflections From Church Leaders*, I have protected the identity of some Church leaders and pastors whom I asked to preview this book pre-publication because of the sensitive nature of the topic under discussion. I am grateful for their contributions which compliment and enrich this book.

Chapter 1

The Message From God Amighty As Received On The 6ᵗʰ January 2014

HOMOSEXUALITY OR GAY RELATIONSHIPS – WHAT DOES GOD ALMIGHTY SAY?

Carnal relationship between men on men – also known as homosexual or gay relationships – what does God Almighty say?

Summary:

The greatest commandment to mankind is given in the gospel of **Luke 10:27 "You shall love the Lord your God with all your heart, with all your soul, with all your strength, and with all your mind and your neighbour as yourself"**. Our overriding duty to men having a carnal relationship with men is to love them. The apostle Paul in 1 Corinthians 13 and verses 4 to 8 describes love: **"Love suffers long, is kind, love does not envy, love does not parade itself, is not puffed up, 5 does not behave rudely, does not seek its own, is not provoked, thinks no evil, 6 does not rejoice in iniquity, but rejoices in the truth; 7 bears all things, believes all things, hopes all things, endures all things. 8 Love never fails…."**

The source of all genuine love is Almighty God for 1 John 4:8 **"He who does not love does not know God, for God is love."** We have an overriding duty to love them and this is expressed in kindness which means being good, giving them equal opportunity in education, employment and all other sources of livelihood and participation in society as these are one hundred percent human, created in the image of God and knowing that when John 3:16 says **"For God so loved the world and gave His only begotten Son, so that whosoever believes in Him should not perish but have everlasting life"** – this scripture applies to them as it applies to the rest of mankind.

The source of the carnal feeling between men and men however is not of God but originates from the wicked one satan. It is driven by demonic forces of satan and a spirit of rebellion and disobedience to the Almighty God. When people attempt to celebrate those feelings, they are joined not by the angels from heaven but by the demonic forces of satan. As we saw above true love does not celebrate, rejoice in or magnify sin or iniquity but true love celebrates, rejoices and magnify the truth of the word of God which is life giving.

Civil partnership acknowledges a practical arrangement between two men or women but does not approve or celebrate it. Gay marriage Act upholds a celebration of unrighteousness and therefore becomes an act of deception by government and not an act of love to people who are gay and lesbian. For this reason, the government should repeal this act as it puts the government at risk of judgement from God. The same applies to adoption of children by gay and lesbian. This is not an act of love to the children or the gay or lesbian couples. This should be abolished as the government risks judgement from God.

The word of God remains the final authority and point of reference as it is the eternal and unshakable truth which does not change. It is spirit and it gives life.

This article sets out why. Covered in this section: *(all quotations from the New King James Version NKJV unless otherwise stated.)*

1.1 The greatest commandments are to love the Lord our God with all our heart, soul, strength and mind and our neighbour as ourselves.
1.2 The authority of the word of God: heaven and earth shall pass away but the word will not pass away. The word is the eternal truth.
1.3 The source of carnal feeling of men to men: what the scriptures say.
1.4 The Parable of the Wheat and the Tares tells us the origin and source of carnal relationships between men and men (and all other forms of evil and rebellion against God) is satan.
1.5 He who made them in the beginning made them male and female: the union between man and woman was decreed and instituted by God himself.
2.6 The relationship between a husband and wife is a mirror image of the relationship between Christ and the Church.
1.7 The grace of God for repentance and salvation has appeared to all – we are all invited to accept it.
1.8 The biblical role of government is to uphold righteousness for righteousness exalts a nation, but sin is a reproach to any people.
1.9 The difference between civil partnership and marriage is celebration. By endorsing gay marriage, the government is upholding celebration of sin, this is not love of people who are gay but deception.

1.10 It is the duty of the church to intercede for the nation and ameliorate God's judgement.

1.11 Word of caution to the child of God – let not this matter consume you and get you out of focus.

1.12 Word to the gay and lesbian – God loves you and so do I – I have a special message for you at the end of which you need to make a choice.

> 1.12.1 To receive His promises you need to understand how to overcome the wicked one.
>
> 1.12.2 To overcome the wicked one you need to understand the nature of satan.
>
> 1.12.3 To overcome the wicked one you need to understand the origins of satan.
>
> 1.12.4 Understanding the believer's victory over satan.
>
> 1.12.5 Understanding the authority of the believer to bind and rebuke satan in the name of the Lord Jesus Christ.
>
> 1.12.6 Understanding the victory over satan through the confession of the blood of the Lord Jesus Christ.
>
> 1.12.7 The Destiny of satan is the lake of fire for all eternity.

1.1. The greatest commandments are to love the Lord our God with all our heart, soul, strength and mind and our neighbour as ourselves.

The greatest commandment to mankind is given in the gospel of **Luke 10:27**

> **"You shall love the Lord your God with all your heart, with all your soul, with all your strength, and with all your mind and your neighbour as yourself".**

Our overriding duty to men having a carnal relationship with men is to love them.

> The apostle Paul in **1 Corinthians 13 and verses 4 to 8** describes love:
>
> **"Love suffers long, is kind, love does not envy, love does not parade itself, is not puffed up,**
>
> **5 does not behave rudely, does not seek its own, is not provoked, thinks no evil,**
>
> **6 does not rejoice in iniquity, but rejoices in the truth;**
>
> **7 bears all things, believes all things, hopes all things, endures all things.**

8 Love never fails...."

The source of all genuine love is Almighty God for **1 John 4:8**

"He who does not love does not know God, for God is love."

We have an overriding duty to love them, and this is expressed in kindness which means being good, giving them equal opportunity in education, employment and all other sources of livelihood and participation in society as these are one hundred percent human, created in the image of God and knowing that when **John 3:16** says:

"For God so loved the world and gave His only begotten Son, so that whosoever believes in Him should not perish but have everlasting life"

– this scripture applies to them as it applies to every single human being on Planet Earth them included.

1.2 The authority of the word of God: heaven and earth shall pass away but the word will not pass away.

The word is the eternal truth. The word of God is eternal, and its truths do not change with time. The word of God is the only truth there is in the absolute sense.

The Lord Jesus in **John 17:17** says **"Sanctify them by your truth, Your word is truth".**

In **John 6:63** the Lord Jesus said **"It is the (Holy) Spirit who gives life; the flesh profits nothing. The words I speak to you are spirit and they are life."**

In **Luke 21** verse **33** the Lord Jesus said, **"Heaven and earth will pass away, but My words will not pass away".**

This scripture says that the word of God is eternal.

In **John 1:1-5** we read

"In the beginning was the Word, and the Word was with God, and the Word was God.

2 He was in the beginning with God.

3 All things were made through Him, and without Him was nothing made that was made.

4 In Him was life, and the life was the light of men.

5 And the light shines in the darkness, and the darkness did not comprehend it."

John 1:14 then says referring to the Lord Jesus Christ **"And the Word became flesh and dwelt among us, and we beheld His glory, the glory as of the only begotten of the Father, full of grace and truth."**

Here we learn that the Lord Jesus Christ is the embodiment of the eternal Word of God, and that word is truth and true love celebrates that word.

In **1 John 5:7** we learn **"For there are three that bear witness in heaven: the Father, the Word and the Holy Spirit."**

The Word of God is the Lord Jesus.

In **Revelations 19:11-16** the scriptures say:

"Now I saw heaven opened, and behold, a white horse. And He who sat on him was called Faithful and True, and in righteousness He judges and makes war.

12 His eyes were like a flame of fire, and on His head were many crowns. He had a name written that no one knew except Himself.

13 He was clothed with a robe dipped in blood, and His name is called the Word of God.

14 And the armies in heaven, clothed in fine linen, white and clean, followed Him on white horses.

15 Now out of His mouth goes a sharp sword, that with it He should strike the nations. And He Himself will rule them with a rod of iron. He Himself treads the winepress of the fierceness and wrath of Almighty God.

16 And He has on His robe and on His thigh a name written: KING OF KINGS AND LORDS OF LORDS".

We notice again here that the Lord Jesus is the Word of God and the executor of the judgement of the Almighty God, backed by the armies of heaven.

1.3 The source of carnal feeling of men to men: what the scriptures say.

The Lord Jesus said in **John 8:32 "And you shall know the truth, and the truth shall make you free."**

It is important that we are able to stand up to speak the truth which shall set free those who choose to be set free by it.

2 Peter 1:16 says **"For we did not follow cunningly devised fables when we made known to you the power and coming of our Lord Jesus Christ, but we were eyewitnesses of His majesty."**

The author writes here as a person who by the grace of God was made an eyewitness of the Lord Jesus Christ and to whom the Lord Jesus has spoken truths about Himself.

Leviticus 18:22 states **"You shall not lie with a male as with a woman. It is an abomination."**

Leviticus 20:13 says: **"If a man lies with a male as he lies with a woman, both of them have committed an abomination".**

The Oxford English Dictionary defines *abominable act* as *"detestable, loathsome, morally reprehensible"* and *abomination* as *"an object of disgust, an odious or degrading habit or act"*.

In **Romans 1:21-27** we read in the holy scriptures:

"Because, although they knew God, they did not glorify Him as God, nor were thankful, but became futile in their thoughts, and their foolish hearts were darkened,

22 professing to be wise, they became fools,

23 and changed the glory of the incorruptible God into an image like corruptible man – and birds and four-footed animals and creeping things.

24 Therefore God also gave them up to uncleanness, in the lusts of their hearts, to dishonour their bodies among themselves,

25 who exchanged the truth of God for a lie, and worshipped and served the creature rather than the Creator, who is blessed forever. Amen.

26 For this reason God gave them up to vile passions. For even their women exchanged the natural use of what is against nature.

27 Likewise also the men, leaving the natural use of the woman, burned in their lust for one another, men with men committing what is shameful, and receiving in themselves the penalty of their error which was due."

Here the word of God states that not being thankful, not acknowledging God as God, failing to give Him the glory, failing to live in humility before God, failure to acknowledge human limitations and living in unbelief can result in one being given up to un-natural affections.

In **1 Corinthians 6:9-11** the scriptures say:

"Do you not know that the unrighteous will not inherit the kingdom of God? Do not be deceived. Neither fornicators, nor idolaters, nor homosexuals, nor sodomites,

10 nor thieves, nor covetous, nor drunkards, nor revilers, nor extortioners will inherit the kingdom of God.

11 And such were some of you. But you were washed, but you were sanctified, but you were justified in the name of the Lord Jesus Christ and by the Spirit of our God.

The above scriptures refer to carnal relationship between man and man as well as women and women and state that they are sin and are done in a state of rebellion to the will of God.

1 Corinthians 9:11 above states that there is available grace to wash by the blood of Jesus, to be sanctified or set apart for God and be justified through repentance, believing in the sacrifice that the Lord Jesus made for mankind when He suffered, died on the cross and rose again from the dead on the third day.

1.4 The Parable of the Wheat and the Tares tells us the origin and source of carnal relationships between men and men (and all other forms of evil and rebellion against God) is satan.

In **Matthew 13:24-30** The scriptures say:

"Another parable He put forth to them, saying: The kingdom of heaven is like a man who sowed good seed in his field;

25 but while men slept, his enemy came and sowed tares among the wheat and went his way.

26 But when the grain had sprouted and produced a crop, then the tares also appeared.

27 So the servants of the owner came and said to him, 'Sir, did you not sow good seed in your field? How then does it have tares?'

28 He said to them, 'An enemy has done this.' The servants said to him, 'Do you want us then to go and gather them up?'

29 But he said, 'No, lest while you gather up the tares you also uproot the wheat with them.

30 Let both grow together until the harvest, and at the time of harvest I will say to the reapers, 'First gather together the tares and bind them in bundles to burn them but gather the wheat into my barn.'"

In verse 36 this parable is explained

> "Then Jesus sent the multitudes away and went into the house. And His disciples came to Him, saying 'Explain to us the parable of the tares of the field.'
>
> 37 He answered and said to them: 'He who sows the seed is the Son of Man.
>
> 38 The field is the world, the good seeds are the sons of the kingdom, but the tares are the sons of the wicked one.
>
> 39 The enemy who sowed them is the devil, the harvest is the end of the age, and the reapers are the angels.
>
> 40 Therefore as the tares are gathered and burned in the fire, so it will be at the end of this age.
>
> 41 The Son of Man will send out His angels and they will gather out of His kingdom all things that offend, and those who practice lawlessness,
>
> 42 and will cast them into the furnace of fire. There will be wailing and gnashing of teeth.
>
> 43 Then the righteous will shine forth as the sun in the kingdom of their Father. He who has ears to hear, let them hear!"

The point of this parable is to explain that there are things, feelings, behaviours, that were not of God's making but are sown by the enemy of God and mankind satan. The carnal feeling of men for men or female for female are from demons, their origin is satan just as all other negative feeling of hate, murder, adultery, stealing, fornication, idolatry and all other forms of sin or rebellion against God.

1.5 He who made them in the beginning made them male and female: the union between man and woman was decreed and instituted by God himself.

In **Matthew 19** verses 3 to 6 we read:

> The Pharisees also came to Him (Lord Jesus) saying to Him, "Is it lawful for a man to divorce his wife for just any reason?"
>
> 4 And He answered and said to them, "Have you not read that He who made them at the beginning 'made them male and female,'
>
> 5 and said, 'For this reason a man shall leave his father and mother and be joined to his wife, and the two shall become one flesh'?

6 So they are no longer two but one flesh. Therefore, what God has joined together, let no man separate."

So, then God made male and female and an arrangement where a man (and the woman) would leave their parents and be joined to become one flesh (two with one common agenda, one purpose and consummated in physical union). The purpose of this arrangement was for them to serve God together, accomplish God's purpose on the earth together and included in that purpose was the multiplication of humanity through bringing up children.

This arrangement therefore had a Godly purpose, with a Godly agenda. God also put true love as the binding force of this arrangement. God valued this arrangement so much that it is an image of the relationship between the Lord Jesus Christ and the Church.

1.6 The relationship between a husband and wife is a mirror image of the relationship between Christ and the Church

In **Ephesians 5:22-32** we read:

> **Wives submit to your own husbands, as to the Lord. And He is the Saviour of the body.**
>
> **23 For the husband is head of the wife, as also Christ is the head of the church; and He is the Saviour of the body.**
>
> **24 Therefore just as the church is subject to Christ, so let the wives be to their own husbands in everything.**
>
> **25 Husbands love your wives, just as Christ also loved the church and gave Himself for her,**
>
> **26 that He might sanctify and cleanse her with the washing of water by the word,**
>
> **27 that He might present her to Himself a glorious church, not having spot or wrinkle or any such thing, but that she should be holy and without blemish.**
>
> **28 So husbands ought to love their own wives as their as their own bodies; he who loves his wife loves himself.**
>
> **29 For no one ever hated his own flesh, but nourishes and cherishes it, just as the Lord does the church.**
>
> **30 For we are members of His body, of His flesh and of His bones.**

> 31 "For this reason a man shall leave his father and mother and be joined to his wife, and the two shall become one flesh." This is great mystery, but I speak concerning Christ and the church.

1.7 The grace of God for repentance and salvation has appeared to all – we are all invited to accept it.

Titus 2:11-15 says:

> For the grace of God that brings salvation has appeared to all men,
>
> 12 teaching us that, denying ungodliness and worldly lusts, we should live soberly, righteously, and godly in this present age,
>
> 13 looking for the blessed hope and glorious appearing of our great God and Saviour Jesus Christ,
>
> 14 who gave Himself for us, that He might redeem us from every lawless deed and purify for Himself His own special people, zealous for good works.
>
> 15 Speak these things, exhort, and rebuke with all authority. Let no one despise you.

The grace of God is the enabling power or force which enables us to receive salvation – this power is available to all – we are invited to accept the word of God, to believe that the Lord Jesus died for us, shed blood that our sins may be forgiven, believe that He rose again from the dead and is alive today, then we are invited to repent (that is agree with the word of God that what it says is right is right and what it says is wrong is wrong) and invite the Lord Jesus to be Lord of our lives.

The following prayer will help you if you pray it sincerely from your heart:

Father in heaven, I thank you for sending your son Jesus Christ to suffer and die for my sins on the cross. I repent of all my sin today. I believe that the Lord Jesus rose again from the dead on the third day. I ask you Lord Jesus to come into my life, to forgive me all my sin, to be my Lord and to make me a child of God. Thank you Lord for hearing my prayer today, thank you for forgiving my sin and for making me a child of God. From today I will live for you. In Jesus's name I pray, Amen.

1.8 The biblical role of government is to uphold righteousness for righteousness exalts a nation, but sin is a reproach to any people.

The word of God says in **Proverbs 14:34**: **Righteousness exalts a nation, but sin is a reproach to any people.**

The word of God goes further to say in **Romans 13:1-2 Let every soul be subject to governing authorities. For there is no authority except from God, and the authorities that exist are appointed by God.**

Governments are therefore appointed ultimately by God to uphold righteousness and help people fulfil the greatest commandment as stated in **Luke 10:27 "You shall love the Lord your God with all your heart, with all your soul, with all your strength, and with all your mind and your neighbour as yourself".**

In doing this the government's functions and judgements will be enhanced by an understanding and revelation of the source and orchestrator of all goodness who is Lord God Almighty who is also the source of all true love and the source of wickedness, evil and deception which is satan. The government's role will also be enhanced by an understanding of righteousness because it is righteousness which exalts a nation, as well as an understanding of sin which is cooperation with the enemy of mankind and the enemy of God called satan who is the source of all evil and wickedness.

1.9 The difference between civil partnership and marriage is celebration. By endorsing gay marriage, the government is upholding celebration of unrighteousness and sin, this is not love of people who are gay but deception.

The equal opportunity policy aims at showing love to all people equally, giving equal opportunity for education, employment, sources of livelihood and respect for personal choices and liberties. Essentially it is an upholding of the commandment to "love your neighbour as you love yourself". All love points towards God and reflects God because God is love as we read in 1 John 4:8. We also saw in **1 Corinthians 13:4 that love is kind**. In other words when one loves one he/she shows acts of kindness to the person they love. Crucially in **1 Corinthians 13:6 love does not rejoice in iniquity but rejoices in the truth.** The Amplified version puts it as **"Love does not rejoice at injustice and unrighteousness but rejoices when right and truth prevail."**

Putting it simply, civil partnerships acknowledge a civil arrangement for the purposes of taxes, understanding accommodation arrangements etc but does not endorse a celebration of unrighteousness and sin. By the Same Sex Marriage Act the government is endorsing a celebration of unrighteousness and sin. This is not love to the person who is gay, but the government is upholding and endorsing a deception from satan. When this celebration is happening demons from satan join in but not angels from heaven. Civil partnerships acknowledge an arrangement without necessarily endorsing it.

By the same token adoption of innocent children by couples in a gay or lesbian relationship is not an act of love to the child, because children were never meant to be raised in such an environment.

1.10 It is the duty of the church to intercede for the nation and ameliorate God's judgement. It is the duty of every true child of God to pray and intercede for the nation to ameliorate God's judgement.

In 1 Timothy 2:1-4 the word of God says:

> "Therefore, I exhort first of all that supplications, prayers, intercessions, and giving of thanks be made for all men,
>
> 2 for kings and all who are in authority, that we may lead quiet and peaceable life in all godliness and reverence.
>
> 3 For this is good and acceptable to God our Saviour,
>
> 4 who desires all men to be saved and come to the knowledge of the truth."

The word of God also says in **2 Chronicles 7:13-14**:

> When I shut up heaven and there is no rain, or command locusts to devour the land, or send a pestilence among my people,
>
> 14 if My people who are called by My name will humble themselves and pray and seek my face and turn from their evil ways, then I will hear from heaven, and will forgive their sin and heal their land.

In **Genesis 18:16-33** Abraham interceded for the city of Sodom begging God for mercy until God agreed not to destroy Sodom if there were found ten righteous people in it.

In the final event God found only one righteous Lot and his family which He rescued and took out of the city before it was destroyed with fire and brimstone which rained from heaven. In Genesis 6 we see the story of how God judged the world with floods in the days of Noah.

Now while God has judged in the past and has threatened judgement, we can only warn things which can result in judgement while the children of God continue to intercede for the nation. There are countless laws and rules which the government has been spot on in doing their God given duty of legislating to protect people. It is however the duty of men of God to warn the government when laws cross the line. The Same Sex Marriage Act according to the word God has spoken to me crosses that line and the government should repeal it. Adoption of children by gay and lesbian couples also crosses that line and should be banned. If the government chooses to ignore these views, the church will continue to intercede for the nation and ask God for mercy but there is a risk of judgement from heaven.

1.11 Word of caution to the child of God – let not this matter consume you and get you out of focus.

It is important that God's children are not consumed by the issue of carnal relationships between men and men or women with women as this is not the greatest challenge facing the child of God today. The greatest challenge is faith, believing the word of God and experiencing His presence, His joy, peace and loving kindness, His mercies and goodness in our lives every day. Seek therefore to experience His goodness for in Exodus 33:19 the word of the Lord says **"I will make all my goodness to pass before you…"**

In **Psalms 34:8** His word says: **"Oh taste and see that the Lord is good; blessed is the man who trusts in Him".**

Psalms 136:1 says: **"Oh give thanks to the Lord, for He is good! For His mercy endures forever".**

Lamentations 3:22-23 says **"Through the Lord's mercies we are not consumed, because His compassions fail not. They are new every morning; great is Your faithfulness".**

When a child of God experiences these he/she can love others unconditionally and impart hope to others.

1.12 Word to the gay and lesbian – God loves you and so do I – I have a special message for you at the end of which you need to make a choice.

The word of God in **John 8:3-11** says:

Then the scribes and Pharisees brought to Him a woman caught in adultery. And when they have sat her in the midst,

4 they said to Him, "Teacher, this woman was caught in adultery, in the very act.

5 Now Moses, in the law, commanded us that such should be stoned. But what do you say?"

6 This they said, testing Him, that they might have something to accuse Him. But Jesus stooped down and wrote on the ground with His finger, as though He did not hear.

7 So when they continued asking Him, He raised Himself up and said to them, "He who is without sin among you, let Him throw a stone at her first,"

8 And again He stooped down and wrote on the ground.

9 Then those who heard it, being convicted by their conscience, went out one by one, beginning with the oldest even to the last. And Jesus was left alone, and the woman standing in the midst.

10 When Jesus had raised Himself up and saw no one but the woman, He said to her, Woman, where are those accusers of yours? Has no one condemned you?"

11 She said "No one, Lord." And Jesus said to her, "Neither do I condemn you; go and sin no more."

Notice here that Jesus refused to condemn this woman. The woman herself however acknowledged her wrong, repented, and confessed Jesus as Lord. She obtained salvation and eternal life.

While the Lord Jesus was on the cross, **Luke 23: 39-43** says:

Then one of the criminals who were hanged blasphemed Him, saying, "If you are the Christ, save Yourself and us."

40 But the other, answering, rebuked him, saying, "Do you not even fear God, seeing you are under the same condemnation?

41 And we indeed justly, for we receive the due reward of our deeds; but this Man has done nothing wrong."

42 Then he said to Jesus, "Lord, remember me when you come into Your kingdom."

43 And Jesus said to him, "Assuredly, I say to you, today you will be with Me in Paradise."

The difference between these two robbers is that one decided to repent and confess Jesus as Lord and the other did not. I implore you to choose the former. You then need to understand how to deal with and overcome the enemy called satan, his nature, his origins, how he was defeated on the cross and his final destiny in the lake of fire.

1.12.1 To receive His promises you need to understand how to overcome the wicked one.

I will dwell on overcoming the wicked one AS IT IS CRITICAL for every child of God to know the enemy we are dealing with, his nature, his origins, the weapons he uses and above all how he was defeated openly and publicly by the Lord Jesus Christ on the cross. In no other area of walking with God is the acquiring of KNOWLEDGE more critical.

1.12.2 To overcome the wicked one you need to understand the nature of satan.

The devil, satan, the wicked one, is described in the word of God as a thief, a murderer, a destroyer, a liar, the father of lies, the accuser of brethren, the deceiver of the whole world, the old serpent, the adversary. The devil is the architect and orchestrator of all sin, all wrongdoing and all evil.

In **John 10:10** the Lord Jesus says **"The thief does not come except to steal and to kill and to destroy. I have come that they may have life and that they may have it more abundantly"**.

In **John 8:44** the Lord Jesus spoke to people seeking to kill Him and said **"You are of your father the devil, and the desires of your father you want to do. He was a murderer from the beginning, and does not stand in the truth, because he has no truth in him. When he speaks a lie, he speaks from his own resources, for he is a liar and the father of it"**.

1 John 3:8 says, **"[But] he who commits sin [who practices evildoing] is of the devil [takes his character from the evil one], for the devil has sinned [violated the divine law] from the beginning. The reason the Son of God was made manifest (visible) was to undo (destroy, loosen, and dissolve) the works the devil [has done]** *(AMP)*".

In **1 Peter 5:8-9** the word of God says **"Be sober, be vigilant, because your adversary the devil walks about like a roaring lion, seeking whom he may devour. Resist him steadfast in the faith, knowing that the same sufferings are experienced by your brotherhood in the world."**

1.12.3 To overcome the wicked one you need to understand the origins of satan.

Satan was created by God and was once a highly decorated angel called Lucifer. Due to pride, he rebelled against God, taking with him a third of the angels of God and was thrown out of heaven and 'fell' to the earth. The other angels who fell with him became demons. His aim is to frustrate every plan and purpose of God on the earth and in mankind.

Isaiah 14:12-17 describes the fall of Lucifer:

> "How are you fallen from heaven, O Lucifer, son of the morning! How are you cut down to the ground, you who weakened the nations!
>
> 13 For you have said in your heart: 'I will ascend into heaven; I will exalt my throne above the stars of God; I will also sit on the mount of the congregation on the farthest side of the north.
>
> 14 I will ascend above the heights of the clouds; I will be like the Most High'.
>
> 15 Yet you shall be brought down to Sheol, to the lowest depth of the Pit,
>
> 16 those who see you will gaze at you and consider you, saying: 'Is this the man who made the earth tremble, who shook kingdoms,
>
> 17 who made the world as a wilderness and destroyed its cities, who did not open the house of his prisoners.'"

In **Revelations 12:3-4** we read:

> "And another sign appeared in heaven: behold a great, fiery red dragon having seven heads and ten horns, and seven diadems on his heads.
>
> 4 His tail drew a third of the stars of heaven and threw them on the earth."

Revelations 12:7-9 says

> "And war broke out in heaven: Michael and his angels fought with the dragon; and the dragon and his angels fought,
>
> 8 but they did not prevail, nor was a place found for them in heaven any longer.
>
> 9 So the great dragon was cast out, that serpent of old, called the devil and *satan*, who deceives the whole world; he was cast to the earth, and his angels were cast out with him."

Ezekiel 28:12-19 describes the beauty and splendour of Lucifer before he fell:

> "Son of man, take up a lamentation for the king of Tyre and say to him, 'Thus says the Lord God: You were the seal of perfection, full of wisdom and perfect in beauty."
>
> 13 You were in Eden, the garden of God; every precious stone was your covering: the sardius, topaz, and diamond, beryl, onyx, and jasper, sapphire, turquoise, and emerald with gold. The workmanship of your timbrels and pipes was prepared for you on the day you were created.
>
> 14 You were the anointed cherub who covers; I established you; you were on the holy mountain of God; you walked back and forth in the midst of fiery stones.
>
> 15 You were perfect in your ways from the day you were created, till iniquity was found in you.
>
> 16 By the abundance of your trading, you became filled with violence within, and you sinned; therefore, I cast you as a profane thing out of the mountain of God; and I destroyed you, O covering cherub, from the midst of the fiery stones.
>
> 17 Your heart was lifted up because of your beauty; you corrupted your wisdom for the sake of your splendour; I cast you to the ground, I laid you before kings, that they may gaze at you.
>
> 18 You defiled your sanctuaries by the multitude of your iniquities, by the iniquity of your trading; therefore, I brought fire from your midst; it devoured you. And I turned you to ashes upon the earth in the sight of all who saw you.
>
> 19 All who knew you among the peoples are astonished at you; you have become a horror and shall be no more forever.'"

The Lord Jesus Christ witnessed this fall of Lucifer. In **Luke 10:18**

> "And He (Lord Jesus Christ) said to them, 'I saw *satan* fall like lightning from heaven'".

1.12.4 Understanding the believer's victory over satan.

Our victory over satan is in believing on the Lord Jesus Christ, the sacrifice He made on the cross when He died for us and rose again from the dead.

In **John 10:10** "The thief comes (referring to satan) **only in order to steal and kill and destroy. I came that they may have and enjoy life and have it in abundance**" (to the full, till it overflows) *(AMP)*.

In **John 3:16**: "For God so greatly loved and dearly prized the world that He (even) gave up His only begotten (unique) Son, so that whosoever believes in (trusts in, clings to, relies on) Him shall not perish (come to destruction, be lost) but have eternal (everlasting) life"(AMP).

In **John 14:6**: "Jesus said to him 'I am the Way, and the Truth and the Life; no one comes to the Father except through me."

The Lord Jesus's agenda was and is to undo the devil's agenda in every person – He came to give life and in abundance, He is the Way the Truth and the Life, He was and is the essence of God's love to the world so that whosoever (anyone of every colour, creed, even religion) believes in Him should not come to destruction (eternal) but have everlasting life.

1 John 4:4 also says:

"You are of God, little children, and have overcome them, because He who is in you is greater than He who is in the world."

When one believes in the Lord Jesus Christ, calls on His name and receives Him as Lord of his life, one gets saved, receives eternal life and is delivered from the devil's principal agenda which is to lead people to eternal separation with God, eternal death and eternal damnation.

The believer also needs to have an understanding and a revelation of the victory that was won for them when the Lord Jesus died on the cross. That satan was disarmed, defeated and made to march down the road naked and was humiliated publicly.

Colossians 2:15 says **"[God] disarmed the principalities and powers that were ranged against us and made a bold display and public example of them, in triumphing over them in Him and in it [the cross]"** *(AMP).*

In **Hebrews 2:14-15** His word also says **"Since, therefore, [these His] children share in flesh and blood [in the physical nature of human beings], He [Himself] in a similar manner partook of the same [nature], that by [going through] death He might bring to nought and make of no affect him who had the power of death—that is, the devil—**

15 And also that He might deliver and completely set free all those who through the [haunting] fear of death were held in bondage throughout the whole course of their lives."

The Lord Jesus Christ therefore by dying on the cross nullified, brought to nought, destroyed, him who had the power of death and set free those who were subjected to bondage all their lives through the fear of death – people who have been living petrified by fear of death are set free when they acknowledge the Lordship of Jesus Christ because He conquered death.

Therefore, He says in **Luke 10:19-20**

> "Behold I give you authority and power to trample upon serpents and scorpions, and [physical and mental strength and ability] over all the power that the enemy [possesses]; and nothing shall in any way hurt you.
>
> 20 Nevertheless, do not rejoice at this, that the spirits are subject to you, but rejoice that your names are enrolled in heaven" *(AMP)*.

1.12.5 Understanding the authority of the believer to bind and rebuke satan in the name of the Lord Jesus Christ.

In **Matthew 12:29** The Lord Jesus referring to satan said **"Or how can one enter a strong man's house and plunder his goods, unless he first binds the strong man? And then he will plunder his house."**

In **Zechariah 3;1-2** the word says

> "Then he showed me Joshua the high priest standing before the Angel of the Lord, and *satan* standing at his right hand to oppose him.
>
> 2 And the Lord said to *satan*, 'The Lord rebukes you, *satan*! The Lord who has chosen Jerusalem rebukes you! Is this not a brand plucked from the fire?'"

The authority that the Lord Jesus Christ gives to the believer gives authority and power to trample or over-run satan and his strategies over one's life or situation, to bind satan and stop him from hindering or interfering in the affairs of one's life and to rebuke satan in the name of and by the authority of the Lord Jesus Christ. It is important for the believer to remember to use this authority often.

1.12.6 Understanding the victory over satan through the confession of the blood of the Lord Jesus Christ.

The believer also needs to know and understand the power of the blood of the Lord Jesus Christ.

In **Exodus 12:7 and 13** says

> "And they shall take some of the blood and put it on the two doorposts and on the lintel of the houses where they shall eat it...
>
> 17 Now the blood shall be a sign for you on the houses where you are. And when I see the blood, I will pass over you; and the plague shall not be on you to destroy you when I strike the land of Egypt."

The blood of the sheep or goats symbolised the blood of the Lord Jesus Christ which was shed on the cross, it is the blood of the Passover. That blood was the purchase price for our redemption from the bondage and all the rights which satan had over mankind because of the sin of Adam and Eve in the Garden of Eden.

1 Peter 1:18-19 says

> "Knowing that you were not redeemed with corruptible things, like gold and silver, from your aimless conduct received by tradition from your fathers,
>
> 19 but with the precious blood of Christ, as of a lamb without blemish and without spot."

In **Revelations 12:10-11** the word says

> "Then I heard a loud voice saying in heaven, 'Now salvation, and strength, and the kingdom of our God, and the power of His Christ have come, for the accuser of our brethren, who accused them day and night, has been cast down.
>
> 11 And they overcame him (*satan*) by the blood of the Lamb (Jesus Christ) and by the word of their testimony, and they did not love their loves to the death.'"

The confession of the blood of the Lord Jesus Christ gives the believer victory and deliverance from the bondage of satan when confessed in faith. The believer has the authority to sprinkle the blood of Lord Jesus Christ over their lives, their loved ones, their possessions etc and make a declaration of victory over satan.

In **Matthew 26:27-28** the word of God reads

> "Then He took the cup, and gave thanks, and gave it to them saying, 'Drink from it, all of you.
>
> 28 For this is My blood of the new covenant, which is shed for many for the remission of sins.'"

The blood of the Lord Jesus that was shed is therefore the seal of the New Covenant. And the confession of that blood gives the believer victory over satan.

1.12.7 The destiny of satan is the lake of fire for all eternity.

The word of God teaches us what will be the final destiny of satan. There is a lake of fire that was prepared for the devil and his angels. It is however critical to know that if one's name is not found in the Lamb's Book of Life, then the same will also be thrown into the lake of fire.

In **Matthew 25:31-32 and 41** The Lord Jesus said:

When the Son of Man comes in His glory, and all the holy angels with Him, then He will sit on the throne of His glory.

32 All the nations will be gathered before Him, and He will separate them one from another, as a shepherd divides his sheep from the goats.

41 Then He will say to those on the left hand, "Depart from Me, you cursed, into the everlasting fire prepared for the devil and his angels.

In **Revelations 19:19-20** the word says

"Then I saw the beast, the kings of the earth, and their armies, gathered together to make war against Him who sat on the horse and against His army.

20 Then the beast was captured, and with him the false prophet who worked signs in his presence, by which he deceived those who received the mark of the beast and those who worshipped his image. These two were cast alive into the lake of fire burning with brimstone."

Revelations 20:10 says

"The devil, who deceived them, was cast into the lake of fire and brimstone where the beast and the false prophet are. And they will be tormented day and night forever and ever.

Revelations 20:11-15 describes the day of judgement and that the destination of evil doers, both small and great, is the lake of fire:

11 Then I saw a great white throne and Him who sat on it, from whose face the earth and the heaven fled away. And there was found no place for them.

12 And I saw the dead, small and great, standing before God, and books were opened. And another book was opened, which is the Book of Life. And the dead were judged according to their works, by the

things which were written in the books.

13 The seas gave up the dead who were in it, and Death and Hades delivered up the dead who were in them. And they were judged, each one according to his works.

14 Then Death and Hades were cast into the lake of fire. This is the second death.

15 And anyone not found written in the Book of Life was cast into the lake of fire.

Here we notice that the day of judgement will be a day of accountability for all – small and great of all the ages.

In **Revelations 21:6-8** we read further:

6 And He said to me, "It is done! I am the Alpha and Omega, the Beginning and the End. I will give of the fountain of the water of life freely to him who thirst.

7 He who overcomes shall inherit all things, and I will be his God and he shall be My son.

8 But the cowardly, unbelieving, abominable, murderers, sexually immoral, sorcerers, idolaters, and all liars shall have their part in the lake which burns with fire and brimstone, which is the second death.

Copyright: *Planet Ministries January 2014*

Chapter 2

Author's Explanatory Notes:
We Need A Standard Of Truth.

We are living in a world today where anybody can say what they want. If a group of people gather outside 10 Downing Street holding banners and placards, people will notice, and policy may change as a result. We need however to define a standard of truth that does not change.

Jesus Christ said in **John 17:17**

Sanctify them by Your truth. Your word is truth.

Please note: the truth is the correct understanding of the word of God. The truth therefore does not change – it is eternal. Understanding of the truth, reveals to you the enemy satan and his working – therefore enabling you to set yourself apart for God. The other words for this are consecration and sanctification. The truth (correct understanding of the word of God that reveals and exposes the enemy satan), is therefore critical for sanctification. Without the truth, you will eat at the dinner table with the enemy satan without realising it!

Jesus Christ said:

Heaven and earth shall pass away but my word shall by no means pass away (Luke 21:33).

His word does not change.

He also said in **John 6:63:**

It is the Spirit who gives life; the flesh profits nothing. The words that I speak to you are spirit, and they are life.

So the word of God is Spirit – it is eternal and life giving.

Jesus Christ is the word of God that was present in the beginning, through whom all things were made.

John 1: 1-4 tells us:

1 In the beginning was the Word, and the Word was with God, and the Word was God.

2 He was in the beginning with God.

3 All things were made through Him, and without Him nothing was made that was made.

4 In Him was life, and the life was the light of men.

Verse 14 then tells us:

And the Word became flesh and dwelt among us, and we beheld His glory, the glory as of the only begotten of the Father, full of grace and truth. (John 1:14).

Jesus Christ, the Son of God was and is the embodiment of the unchangeable word of God which is eternal, which is Spirit and life giving. That is why His word also tells us in **Revelations 19:13:**

He was clothed with a robe dipped in blood, and His name is called The Word of God.

Jesus Christ, does not change as God does not change:

Malachi 3:6 tells us:

For I am the LORD, I do not change;

Therefore, you are not consumed, O sons of Jacob.

Hebrews 13:8 also tells us:

Jesus Christ is the same yesterday, today, and forever.

The standard of truth must be the word of God correctly understood.

Chapter 3

Author's Explanatory Notes: We Need Love And Compassion For Gay People.

When one wakes up feeling for a person of the same sex as they should feel for the opposite sex, it is a trap, it is deception of the enemy satan. The scriptures tell us the author of this trap is the enemy satan.

This feeling is sown by the enemy satan, as are other forms of sin and disobedience to God such as murder, stealing, lying, adultery, fornication etc.

The parable of the wheat and tares explain that the origin of these acts is satan.

It is clear this is sin. The male organ was never meant to find its way into the rectum, where faeces are found.

We need however to separate the person from the act. The person needs love and compassion. This means kindness and equal opportunity. This means we must give them a chance to repent in their own time. We should not pre-maturely judge them. Jesus Christ refused to judge the woman that was caught in adultery – in the very act. Why? He knew that His mission was to die for the sin of the world including this woman – she needed to access forgiveness through repentance. That is why the scriptures tell us in **John 8:10-11:**

> 'When Jesus had raised Himself up and saw no one but the woman, He said to her, "Woman, where are those accusers of yours? Has no one condemned you?"
>
> 11 She said, "No one, Lord."
>
> And Jesus said to her, "Neither do I condemn you; go and sin no more."

His word teaches us in **Hebrews 9:27**

And as it is appointed for men to die once, but after this the judgment.

Everyone needs to be given a chance to repent – while they still have breath in them. Until their last breath, there is still a chance for repentance. Our duty before then is to love them and tell them the truth – as you turn to God in repentance, you will find that God is not angry with you, He is not even in a bad mood, He does not condemn you, He sent His Son Jesus Christ to suffer and die for you. He rose again and is alive today. God wants you to make it to heaven – as he does for every single person on the Planet Earth. The route to forgiveness of sin for all is repentance.

Repentance is changing your mind and agreeing with God as to what is right and wrong. Repentance is not grovelling, coming to God, and begging for forgiveness until you feel good – no – repentance is changing your mind, changing allegiance and coming to God. Jesus Christ has already dealt with sin. In the process you need to access the help of Jesus Christ directly, to be transformed by Him as you commit your life to Him, acknowledge the sacrifice He made when He suffered and died on the cross, believe that God raised Him from the dead and He is alive today. You then need to call upon His name and acknowledge Him as Lord of your life.

The robber on the cross made it to heaven, by repenting before his last breath. Jesus Christ said to him:

Today you shall be with Me in paradise. *(Luke 23:43).*

Chapter 4

Author's Explanatory Notes: Why Same Sex Marriage Works Against Gay People.

Same sex marriage puts the gay at bigger risk of perishing in hell, this is not the will of God.

The scriptures tell us in **John 3:16-17:**

For God so loved the world that He gave His only begotten Son, that whoever believes in Him should not perish but have everlasting life.

17 For God did not send His Son into the world to condemn the world, but that the world through Him might be saved.

His word teaches us further in **Luke 24: 46-47: Then He said to them,**

"Thus it is written, and thus it was necessary for the Christ to suffer and to rise from the dead the third day,

47 and that repentance and remission of sins should be preached in His name to all nations, beginning at Jerusalem.

His word further tells us in **Romans 3:23:**

For all have sinned and fall short of the glory of God.

The critical point here is that – all have sinned and come short of the glory of God. It is the will of God that all may be saved, through believing on the sacrifice made by Jesus Christ when He shed His blood and died for the redemption of mankind.

The route to salvation is through repentance, changing your mind, acknowledging that mistake and turning to God.

His word says in **Luke 13:3: I tell you, no; but unless you repent you will all likewise perish.**

Celebrating same sex marriage brings one further from repentance, sucks one deeper into co-operating with the enemy satan and hinders repentance, makes it harder for repentance to happen. It therefore puts the gay person more at risk of perishing in hell.

Jesus Christ died for all, gay and straight. God distinguishes between the person He loves, the person He sent His Son Jesus Christ to die for, and the sin. He loves the person, but He hates the sin. The route to access forgiveness is though repentance and believing on the sacrifice made by Jesus Christ. Following that one needs renewal of the mind by the correct understanding of the word of God, to put off the old person and put on the new man.

In **Ephesians 4:22-24** we read:

22 that you put off, concerning your former conduct, the old man which grows corrupt according to the deceitful lusts,

23 and be renewed in the spirit of your mind,

24 and that you put on the new man which was created according to God, in true righteousness and holiness.

Following repentance and acknowledging Jesus Christ as Lord you need to set yourself apart for God – consecration – this a decision one needs to make followed by a declaration – "I am yours Lord with all that I am I give my life to You, Lord You can have me, do your will in my life and accomplish your purpose through me."

Repentance means you make a stand against sin, you change your behaviour, you change your lifestyle from that point onwards.

The decision to repent is made – it may take deliberating, thinking deeply, consulting – but once made – it is made in an instant. One makes up his mind, this is not right, this was deception, I do not want it anymore, I have changed my mind. This decision is made at a point in time-stick to it and acknowledge the risen Jesus Christ as Lord. Make a decision to follow Him.

You ask for the power of the Holy Spirit to fill and empower you (see Vessels of Excellence – by the same author).

You then need teaching of the word of God to renew and transform the way you think – in this process you are putting off the old person and putting on the new person. This is a process, and you need to allow time for transformation and renewal.

Chapter 5

Author's Explanatory Notes: Civil Partnership Act And Same Sex Marriage Act -Why The Latter Crosses The Line From Heaven.

The main difference is celebration – the celebration of Same Sex Marriage is joined by the enemy satan and demons not by angels from heaven. It is a celebration done in rebellion to Almighty God. As such it sucks one deeper and deeper into co-operating with the enemy satan and draws one further and further away from repentance.

Civil Partnership Act acknowledges an arrangement made between two consenting adults for the purposes of tax, accommodation arrangements etc. It does not endorse the arrangement nor celebrates it.

The Same Sex Marriage Act purports to celebrate this arrangement. In this situation the government is failing in its fundamental duty in safeguarding individuals from co-operating with the wicked one satan. It is failing to expose deception of the enemy satan.

The equal opportunity policy aims at showing love to all people equally, giving equal opportunity for education, employment, sources of livelihood and respect for personal choices and liberties. Essentially it is an upholding of the commandment to "love your neighbour as you love yourself". All love points towards God and reflects God because **God is love** as we read in 1 John 4:8.

We also saw in **1 Corinthians 13:4 that love is kind**. In other words when one loves one, they show acts of kindness to the person they love. Crucially in **1 Corinthians 13:6 love does not rejoice in iniquity but rejoices in the truth.** The Amplified version puts it as

> "Love does not rejoice at injustice and unrighteousness but rejoices when right and truth prevail."

The word of God teaches us in **Proverbs 14:34:**

Righteousness exalts a nation, but sin is a reproach to any people.

Reproach is to express disappointment or displeasure for conduct that is blameworthy or in need of amendment.

When Almighty God shows displeasure and disappointment in a nation – that puts the nation at risk of judgement from God.

Chapter 6

Author's Explanatory Notes: The Role Of Government In God's Agenda For Mankind.

The word of God says in **Proverbs 14:34**:

Righteousness exalts a nation, but sin is a reproach to any people.

The word of God goes further to say **in Romans 13:1**:

Let every soul be subject to governing authorities. For there is no authority except from God, and the authorities that exist are appointed by God.

Daniel 2:20-21 tells us:

Daniel answered and said:

"Blessed be the name of God forever and ever,

For wisdom and might are His.

And He changes the times and the seasons;

He removes kings and raises up kings;

He gives wisdom to the wise

And knowledge to those who have understanding.

Governments are therefore appointed ultimately by God to uphold righteousness and help people fulfil the greatest commandment as stated in **Luke 10:27**

"You shall love the Lord your God with all your heart, with all your soul, with all your strength, and with all your mind and your neighbour as yourself".

In doing this the government's functions and judgements will be enhanced by an understanding and revelation of the source and orchestrator of all goodness who is Lord God Almighty who is also the source of all true love and that the source of evil and wickedness is the enemy satan. The government's role will also be enhanced by an understanding of righteousness because it is righteousness which exalts a nation. The government's role is equally enhanced by an understanding of the workings of the enemy of mankind and the enemy of God, satan in the lives of people. The enemy satan is the source of all evil and wickedness. Sin is co-operating with the enemy satan.

When a government endorses unrighteousness and sin, that act disempowers Almighty God and results in judgement. Judgement is when God allows the enemy to inflict pain on people that results in repentance. Judgement also occurs when Almighty God is disempowered to protect because of sin. When God speaks and releases His wisdom, the most prudent thing for the leaders to do is to obey that instruction. In this case God has spoken clearly and it is incumbent on the government to act.

Chapter 7

Author's Explanatory Notes:
The Duty Of The Church To Intercede For The Nation And Ameliorate Judgement.

We saw in Chapter 1 Section 1:10 that it is the duty of every child of God to intercede for the nation to ameliorate judgement.

The first point here is that God sometimes judges His people. We see in scripture repeatedly that when the children of Israel sinned, God judged them. Often this judgement came in the form of being defeated by their enemies, being taken into captivity and sometimes people being killed.

Let's look at some examples.

We all know of the judgement of Pharaoh with ten plagues when he refused to let the children of Israel go. The last of these was the death of the first born following which Pharaoh let the children of Israel go.

In **Exodus 12:29-32** we read:

> **29 And it came to pass at midnight that the LORD struck all the firstborn in the land of Egypt, from the firstborn of Pharaoh who sat on his throne to the firstborn of the captive who was in the dungeon, and all the firstborn of livestock.**
>
> **30 So, Pharaoh rose in the night, he, all his servants, and all the Egyptians; and there was a great cry in Egypt, for there was not a house where there was not one dead.**
>
> **31 Then he called for Moses and Aaron by night, and said, "Rise, go out from among my people, both you and the children of Israel. And go, serve the LORD as you have said.**
>
> **32 Also take your flocks and your herds, as you have said, and be gone; and bless me also."**

In **Jeremiah 40:3** Jerusalem was besieged by king Nebuchadnezzar because the people of Israel had disregarded the voice of God, we read:

Now the LORD has brought it and has done just as He said. Because you people have sinned against the LORD, and not obeyed His voice, therefore this thing has come upon you.

Notice here that God sent a prophet Jeremiah to explain the wrong they had done and why calamity had come upon them.

In **Ezra 5:12** we read: **But because our fathers provoked the God of heaven to wrath, He gave them into the hand of Nebuchadnezzar king of Babylon, the Chaldean, who destroyed this temple and carried the people away to Babylon.**

Ezra the scribe here explained that when their forefathers disobeyed God, not only did He give them into the hand of King Nebuchadnezzar but it also led to the destruction of the temple which had been built by King Solomon in Jerusalem.

In Judges we notice how the Lord delivered Israel into the hands of the Midianites because they had sinned against the Lord in that they had worshipped the idol gods of the Amorites. When they cried out to the Lord, He sent a prophet to remind them where they had sinned.

We read in **Judges 6:7-10**

And it came to pass, when the children of Israel cried out to the LORD because of the Midianites,

8 that the LORD sent a prophet to the children of Israel, who said to them, "Thus says the LORD God of Israel: 'I brought you up from Egypt and brought you out of the house of bondage;

9 and I delivered you out of the hand of the Egyptians and out of the hand of all who oppressed you, and drove them out before you and gave you their land.

10 Also, I said to you, "I am the LORD your God; do not fear the gods of the Amorites, in whose land you dwell." But you have not obeyed My voice.'"

When King Saul sinned, God sent a prophet Samuel to explain to him where he had gone wrong. We read in **1 Samuel 22-25:**

22 So, Samuel said:

"Has the LORD as great delight in burnt offerings and sacrifices,

As in obeying the voice of the LORD?

Behold, to obey is better than sacrifice,

And to heed than the fat of rams.

23 For rebellion is as the sin of witchcraft,

And stubbornness is as iniquity and idolatry.

Because you have rejected the word of the LORD,

He also has rejected you from being king."

24 Then Saul said to Samuel, "I have sinned, for I have transgressed the commandment of the LORD and your words, because I feared the people and obeyed their voice.

25 Now therefore, please pardon my sin, and return with me, that I may worship the LORD."

Here Saul said I transgressed the commandment of the Lord because I feared the people and obeyed their voice. It is better to obey the voice of God rather than fear the voice of people who often do not know what is good for them in the long run.

When Almighty God points out a deception from the enemy satan, as in this instance, of the Same Sex Marriage Act, it is incumbent on leaders to take heed and protect people.

The other point of note here is that God on all three occasions sent a prophet to the King and to the people with a word from God. On each occasion judgement from God had followed disobedience.

Please notice that while God's judgement can be by His direct action from heaven as was the case of Noah's floods, judgements in Egypt, as well as the destruction of Sodom and Gomorrah, often it is by God withholding His help to His people so that they are defeated by their enemies.

In **Deuteronomy 31:16-30** we read:

And the LORD said to Moses: "Behold, you will rest with your fathers; and this people will rise and play the harlot with the gods of the foreigners of the land, where they go to be among them, and they will forsake Me and break My covenant which I have made with them.

17 Then My anger shall be aroused against them in that day, and I will forsake them, and I will hide My face from them, and they shall be devoured. And many evils and troubles shall befall them, so that they will say in that day, Have not these evils come upon us because our God is not among us?'

18 And I will surely hide My face in that day because of all the evil which they have done, in that they have turned to other gods.

19 "Now therefore, write down this song for yourselves, and teach it to the children of Israel; put it in their mouths, that this song may be a witness for Me against the children of Israel.

20 When I have brought them to the land flowing with milk and honey, of which I swore to their fathers, and they have eaten and filled themselves and grown fat, then they will turn to other gods and serve them; and they will provoke Me and break My covenant.

21 Then it shall be, when many evils and troubles have come upon them, that this song will testify against them as a witness; for it will not be forgotten in the mouths of their descendants, for I know the inclination of their behaviour today, even before I have brought them to the land of which I swore to give them."

22 Therefore Moses wrote this song the same day and taught it to the children of Israel.

23 Then He inaugurated Joshua the son of Nun, and said, "Be strong and of good courage; for you shall bring the children of Israel into the land of which I swore to them, and I will be with you."

24 So it was, when Moses had completed writing the words of this law in a book, when they were finished,

25 that Moses commanded the Levites, who bore the ark of the covenant of the LORD, saying:

26 "Take this Book of the Law, and put it beside the ark of the covenant of the LORD your God, that it may be there as a witness against you;

27 for I know your rebellion and your stiff neck. If today, while I am yet alive with you, you have been rebellious against the LORD, then how much more after my death?

28 Gather to me all the elders of your tribes, and your officers, that I may speak these words in their hearing and call heaven and earth to witness against them.

29 For I know that after my death you will become utterly corrupt, and turn aside from the way which I have commanded you. And evil will befall you in the latter days, because you will do evil in the sight of the LORD, to provoke Him to anger through the work of your hands."

30 Then Moses spoke in the hearing of all the assembly of Israel the words of this song until they were ended.

We notice here in verses 16-18 when the people forsake Me and break My covenant, My anger shall be aroused against them and I will forsake them and hide My face from them, will forsake them and they shall be devoured and many evils and troubles will befall them. Often sin results in God withholding help as a way of judgement.

We notice the same in Deuteronomy 32:15-20:

But Jeshurun grew fat and kicked;

You grew fat, you grew thick,

You are obese!

Then he forsook God who made him,

And scornfully esteemed the Rock of his salvation.

16 They provoked Him to jealousy with foreign gods;

With abominations they provoked Him to anger.

17 They sacrificed to demons, not to God,

To gods they did not know,

To new gods, new arrivals

That your fathers did not fear.

18 Of the Rock who begot you, you are unmindful,

And have forgotten the God who fathered you.

19 "And when the LORD saw it, He spurned them,

Because of the provocation of His sons and His daughters.

20 And He said: 'I will hide My face from them,

I will see what their end will be,

For they are a perverse generation,

Children in whom is no faith.

Notice in verse 19 – when the Lord saw it, He spurned them. Now, to spurn is to reject with disdain or contempt. The King James Version says *He arbored them* – again meaning to regard with disgust, to detest, loathe, hate, scorn, abominate.

Verse 20 goes further to say – I will hide My face from them – which refers to withdrawal of the help of God. This is judgement from God.

Prayers of intercession by the saints ameliorates judgement from God.

When Abraham interceded for Sodom, he asked God not to destroy it if he found ten righteous people and God agreed.

We read in **Genesis 18:30-33:**

30 Then he said, "Let not the Lord be angry, and I will speak: Suppose thirty should be found there?"

So He said, "I will not do it if I find thirty there."

31 And he said, "Indeed now, I have taken it upon myself to speak to the Lord: Suppose twenty should be found there?"

So He said, "I will not destroy it for the sake of twenty."

32 Then he said, "Let not the Lord be angry, and I will speak but once more: Suppose ten should be found there?"

And He said, "I will not destroy it for the sake of ten."

33 So the LORD went His way as soon as He had finished speaking with Abraham; and Abraham returned to his place.

In the end, God could not find ten righteous people in Sodom, but found one, Lot and his family whom because Abraham had interceded, were rescued from Sodom before it was destroyed with fire and brimstone from heaven.

In Numbers, we read the story of how Almighty God was angry at the children of Israel in the wilderness because of their unbelief. God was so angry that if it were not for the intercession of Moses, He would have destroyed the whole nation and start a new nation through Moses. Almighty God relented and forgave.

Numbers 14:11-24 reads:

11 Then the LORD said to Moses: "How long will these people reject Me? And how long will they not believe Me, with all the signs which I have performed among them?

12 I will strike them with the pestilence and disinherit them, and I will make of you a nation greater and mightier than they."

13 And Moses said to the LORD: "Then the Egyptians will hear it, for by Your might You brought these people up from among them,

14 and they will tell it to the inhabitants of this land. They have heard that You, LORD, are among these people; that You, LORD, are seen face to face and Your cloud stands above them, and You go before them in a pillar of cloud by day and in a pillar of fire by night.

15 Now if You kill these people as one man, then the nations which have heard of Your fame will speak, saying,

16 'Because the LORD was not able to bring these people to the land which He swore to give them, therefore He killed them in the wilderness.'

17 And now, I pray, let the power of my Lord be great, just as You have

spoken, saying,

18 The LORD is longsuffering and abundant in mercy, forgiving iniquity and transgression; but He by no means clears the guilty, visiting the iniquity of the fathers on the children to the third and fourth generation.'

19 Pardon the iniquity of this people, I pray, according to the greatness of Your mercy, just as You have forgiven this people, from Egypt even until now."

20 Then the LORD said: "I have pardoned, according to your word;

21 but truly, as I live, all the earth shall be filled with the glory of the LORD—

22 because all these men who have seen My glory and the signs which I did in Egypt and in the wilderness, and have put Me to the test now these ten times, and have not heeded My voice,

23 they certainly shall not see the land of which I swore to their fathers, nor shall any of those who rejected Me see it.

24 But My servant Caleb, because he has a different spirit in him and has followed Me fully, I will bring into the land where he went, and his descendants shall inherit it.

Please note that all the children of Israel who were 20 years and above when they left Egypt perished in the wilderness except for Joshua and Caleb who entered the promised land. The rest died of a plague in the wilderness, and this was Almighty God's judgement.

We read this in the same chapter of Numbers from verses 26-38 as follows:

26 And the LORD spoke to Moses and Aaron, saying,

27 "How long shall I bear with this evil congregation who complain against Me? I have heard the complaints which the children of Israel make against Me.

28 Say to them, 'As I live,' says the LORD, 'just as you have spoken in My hearing, so I will do to you:

29 The carcasses of you who have complained against Me shall fall in this wilderness, all of you who were numbered, according to your entire number, from twenty years old and above.

30 Except for Caleb the son of Jephunneh and Joshua the son of Nun, you shall by no means enter the land which I swore I would make you dwell in.

31 But your little ones, whom you said would be victims, I will bring in, and they shall know the land which you have despised.

32 But as for you, your carcasses shall fall in this wilderness.

33 And your sons shall be shepherds in the wilderness forty years, and bear the brunt of your infidelity, until your carcasses are consumed in the wilderness.

34 According to the number of the days in which you spied out the land, forty days, for each day you shall bear your guilt one year, namely forty years, and you shall know My rejection.

35 I the LORD have spoken this. I will surely do so to all this evil congregation who are gathered together against Me. In this wilderness they shall be consumed, and there they shall die.' "

36 Now the men whom Moses sent to spy out the land, who returned and made all the congregation complain against him by bringing a bad report of the land,

37 those very men who brought the evil report about the land, died by the plague before the LORD.

38 But Joshua the son of Nun and Caleb the son of Jephunneh remained alive, of the men who went to spy out the land.

In the book of **Jonah Chapter 3:1-10** we read:

Now the word of the LORD came to Jonah the second time, saying,

2 "Arise, go to Nineveh, that great city, and preach to it the message that I tell you."

3 So Jonah arose and went to Nineveh, according to the word of the LORD. Now Nineveh was an exceedingly great city, a three-day journey in extent.

4 And Jonah began to enter the city on the first day's walk. Then he cried out and said, "Yet forty days, and Nineveh shall be overthrown!"

5 So the people of Nineveh believed God, proclaimed a fast, and put on sackcloth, from the greatest to the least of them.

6 Then word came to the king of Nineveh; and he arose from his throne and laid aside his robe, covered himself with sackcloth and sat in ashes.

7 And he caused it to be proclaimed and published throughout Nineveh by the decree of the king and his nobles, saying,

Let neither man nor beast, herd nor flock, taste anything; do not let them eat, or drink water.

8 But let man and beast be covered with sackcloth, and cry mightily to God; yes, let every one turn from his evil way and from the violence that is in his hands.

9 Who can tell if God will turn and relent, and turn away from His fierce anger, so that we may not perish?

10 Then God saw their works, that they turned from their evil way; and God relented from the disaster that He had said He would bring upon them, and He did not do it.

When the people of Nineveh including the King took heed to the voice of God that was brought to them by Prophet Jonah and repented, judgement on the city was averted. God relented when He saw that the people returned from their evil ways.

Amos 3:7 tells us:

Surely the Lord GOD does nothing,
unless He reveals His secret to His servants the prophets.

Yes, Almighty God has revealed His secrets in the past and He continues to do so in our generation.

We need to note the following from these examples from the word of God:

1. God reveals things to His prophets as He did to Abraham before Sodom was destroyed, to Samuel before Saul was rejected as king, to Moses before judgement in the wilderness, to Jeremiah before Nebuchadnezzar besieged Jerusalem, to Jonah who preached to the city of Nineveh.

2. In the case of Jonah, people of Nineveh repented, they headed the voice of the prophet and God's judgement was averted altogether.

3. Judgement from God can take the form of direct action from God as in the case of Egypt when the plagues and death of the first born were a result of direct action from God, Sodom and Gomorrah when fire and brimstone came from heaven and as in the days of Noah when Almighty God caused floods to come upon the earth.

4. Judgement from God can also take the form of God forsaking and hiding His face from the people, which means God withholding His help resulting in His people being defeated by their enemies or allowing evil to befall them.

5. It is important for the church to continue to intercede on behalf of the nation and the nations to ameliorate judgement – ultimately it is obedience that will avert judgement altogether.

6. When God speaks it is important for the people to take note: in this case Almighty God has spoken and it is incumbent on people including the government leaders to take note.

7. The author believes that there are events which have happened up and down the country of the United Kingdom (and other nations of the world who have endorsed Gay marriage) which would not have happened if people and the government had taken note of the voice from Almighty God.

Chapter 8

Author's Exploratory Notes: The Benefits Of Repealing Same Sex Marriage Act.

The benefits of repealing the same sex marriage act:
- Brings back the presence of God on to the streets of the nation – this will result in more protection.
- Reduces the risks of judgement from heaven.
- Facilitates repentance and salvation of gay people.

He who made them in the beginning made them male and female and He blessed them and gave them a command to be fruitful and multiply.

In Genesis 1:26-28 His word tells us;

26 Then God said, "Let Us make man in Our image, according to Our likeness; let them have dominion over the fish of the sea, over the birds of the air, and over the cattle, over all the earth and over every creeping thing that creeps on the earth."

27 So God created man in His own image; in the image of God He created him; male and female He created them.

28 Then God blessed them, and God said to them, "Be fruitful and multiply; fill the earth and subdue it; have dominion over the fish of the sea, over the birds of the air, and over every living thing that moves on the earth."

God created them male and female, the plan was always male and female. The mission was to be fruitful and multiply, to fill the earth and subdue it.

In Genesis 2:21-24 we read:

21 And the LORD God caused a deep sleep to fall on Adam, and he slept; and He took one of his ribs, and closed up the flesh in its place.

> 22 Then the rib which the LORD God had taken from man He made into a woman, and He brought her to the man.
>
> 23 And Adam said:
>
> "This is now bone of my bones
>
> And flesh of my flesh;
>
> She shall be called Woman,
>
> Because she was taken out of Man."
>
> 24 Therefore a man shall leave his father and mother and be joined to his wife, and they shall become one flesh.
>
> And they were both naked, the man and his wife, and were not ashamed.

Here we note – therefore a man shall live his father and mother and be joined to his wife and the two shall become one flesh.

Jesus Christ affirmed it in Matthew 19:4-5

> 4 And He answered and said to them, "Have you not read that He who made them at the beginning made them male and female,'
>
> 5 and said, For this reason a man shall leave his father and mother and be joined to his wife, and the two shall become one flesh'?

We read the same scripture in Mark 10:6-8.

The plan and design of God from the beginning was for marriage to be between man and woman.

In **Ephesians 5:25-33** we read:

> Husbands, love your wives, just as Christ also loved the church and gave Himself for her,
>
> 26 that He might sanctify and cleanse her with the washing of water by the word,
>
> 27 that He might present her to Himself a glorious church, not having spot or wrinkle or any such thing, but that she should be holy and without blemish.
>
> 28 So husbands ought to love their own wives as their own bodies; he who loves his wife loves himself.
>
> 29 For no one ever hated his own flesh, but nourishes and cherishes it, just as the Lord does the church.
>
> 30 For we are members of His body, of His flesh and of His bones.

31 "For this reason a man shall leave his father and mother and be joined to his wife, and the two shall become one flesh."

32 This is a great mystery, but I speak concerning Christ and the church.

33 Nevertheless let each one of you in particular so love his own wife as himself, and let the wife see that she respects her husband.

We notice here that husbands are instructed to love their wives as Christ loved the church. They are instructed to lay down their lives for their wives. We also notice that the mystery of this relationship is a mirror image of the relationship between Christ and the church.

We notice therefore that the relationship between a man and a woman in marriage was ordained by God Himself and He put Himself at the centre of it.

What we are seeing in gay relationships is a deceptive counterfeit, designed by the enemy satan, to put people into bondage and in rebellion against God.

Chapter 9

There Is A Way Back For The Gay And Lesbian.

We know that a lot of times events in early childhood orchestrated by the enemy satan results in hurt and mistrust of the opposite sex and may result in feelings of gay or lesbian. For example, 85% of lesbians were abused or molested as children and 40% of gay men were seduced or molested by older gay men when they were younger.

There is a path back for you by repenting and believing on Jesus Christ.

Repentance is not grovelling in dirt and condemning yourself until you feel you have sufficiently earned God's forgiveness.

The word repentance in the New Testament is the Greek word metanoia, which simply means "a change of mind." Meta means "change" and noia refers to your mind.

Repentance then means changing your mind because of right believing that leads to inward heart transformation.

It is right believing that brings about true repentance (change of mind) and hence genuine transformation. It is impossible to truly repent, to experience Jesus, His love, His grace, and His power and to allow Him to transform your mind and your belief system – and still remain the same.

Many man-centred teachings on contrition and repentance can sound so good, but in reality trap people in a cycle of defeat and hypocrisy. The truth is that if you are a new creation in Christ, you already hate sin and the wrongdoing. It vexes your soul and you are looking for a way out of your bondage.

The repentance you need – the change of mind you need – is to know that God has *already forgiven you*, Jesus Christ when He shed His blood and died, paid the price for your forgiveness.

His word says in **2 Corinthians 5:21**

For He made Him who knew no sin to be sin for us, that we might become the righteousness of God in Him.

1 Corinthians 6:11 tells us:

And such were some of you. But you were washed, but you were sanctified, but you were justified in the name of the Lord Jesus and by the Spirit of our God.

You therefore need to stop condemning yourself and walk in His righteous identity to new levels of victory over sin.

When wrong thoughts come into your mind, the repentance you need is to know that those thoughts do not belong to you. Repentance in this situation is not beating yourself up over those thoughts, no, give them no room to flourish by ignoring them while you continue to be established and secure in your new identity in Christ. Fill your mind with His thoughts, His living Word, His love, His peace and His joy.

2 Corinthians 5:17 tells us:

Therefore, if anyone is in Christ, he is a new creation; old things have passed away; behold, all things have become new.

Make this your prayer and declaration:

Thank you Lord that I am a new creation in Jesus Christ, old things have passed away, my old way of life, old ways of thinking, old friends and social associations – everything is now new.

John 1:12 tells us:

But as many as received Him, to them He gave the authority (power, privilege, right) to become children of God, that is to those who believe in (adhere to, trust in, rely on) His name: who owe their birth neither to bloods nor will of the flesh(that physical impulse) nor the will of man (that of a natural father) but to God. [they are born of God] *(AMP)*.

Make this your prayer and declaration:

I received Jesus Christ as my Lord, I have been given the authority, the right and the privilege to be a child of God. I am now born again into the household of God. I belong to Jesus Christ. I am married to Jesus Christ in my spirit.

Romans 8:17 tells us:

For you did not receive the spirit of bondage again to fear, but you received the Spirit of adoption by whom we cry out, "Abba, Father."

Make this your prayer and declaration:

Thank you Lord that I did not receive the spirit of bondage to fear, but I received the spirit of adoption, I have been adopted by Jesus Christ in me to become a member of the household of God. I can now say to you God, you are my Father.

Romans 5:1 tells us:

Therefore, having been justified by faith, we have peace with God through our Lord Jesus Christ.

Make this your prayer and your confession:

Thank you Lord that I have been justified by faith, I am now at peace with God through my Lord Jesus Christ.

Romans 8:1-2 tells us:

There is therefore now no condemnation to those who are in Christ Jesus, who do not walk according to the flesh, but according to the Spirit. For the law of the Spirit of life in Christ Jesus has made me free from the law of sin and death.

Make this your prayer and your confession:

Thank you Lord Jesus that there is now no condemnation for me who is in Christ Jesus, because I no longer walk, according to the flesh, obeying the dictates of the flesh, but I now walk and live according to the Spirit of Jesus Christ because the law of the Spirit of life in Jesus Christ has set me free from the law of sin and death.

Homosexuality is not a sin which God cannot forgive. You must be willing to sacrifice your bodily desires and be identified deeply with Jesus Christ. There is freedom and complete healing found in a deep and radical obedience to Jesus Christ. You need to face and deal with the wounds and sins of the past, be open about them and find people you trust whom you can confide in. You may need prayer for deliverance. The key however will be in setting yourself apart or consecrating yourself for Jesus Christ.

This prayer outline will help you, but you need to submit yourself freely and willingly to the will and Lordship of Jesus Christ. Not under any form of cohesion or pressure. It is a prayer of consecration. When you are ready:

I am yours Lord with all that I am and with all that I am not, I give myself to You, You can have me Lord, the whole of me, satan I reject you, and every spirit of bondage, I command you in the name of Jesus Christ to let me go and serve God. I was bought by the blood of Jesus Christ and I speak the covering of the blood of Jesus Christ upon my life.

You need to understand that you are three in one – you have a spirit – the part of you that was made in the image of God, which is eternal.

You have a soul – which is your mind and the seat of the emotions, intellect, will and conscience.

Your intellect – the part of you that reasons and thinks things through-

Your will – the part of you that makes decisions.

Your conscience – the part of you that discerns right and wrong.

Your emotions – the part of you that loves or hates, feels happy or sad etc.

And you have the physical body.

You need to discern the truth and decide with your mind and intellect to follow Jesus Christ. Jesus Christ is a person, but He is also called the Word of God (Revelations 19:13). As you allow your mind to be transformed with the word of God, correctly understood, your emotions will follow suit. The word of God correctly understood is called the truth. It is the truth that will set you free.

That is why Jesus Christ said in **John 8:31-32:**

Then Jesus said to those Jews who believed Him, "If you abide in My word, you are My disciples indeed. And you shall know the truth, and the truth shall make you free."

It is also the truth that sanctifies or enables you to be set apart for God because the truth gives you a revelation of the working of the enemy satan. In other words, the truth shows you the line you should not cross – because as you cross that line you will going into enemy territory.

That is why Jesus Christ said in **John 17:17:**

Sanctify them by Your truth. Your word is truth.

The enemy satan is a liar and the father of all lying.
Jesus said in John 8:44:

You are of your father the devil, and the desires of your father you want to do. He was a murderer from the beginning, and does not stand in the truth, because there is no truth in him. When he speaks a lie, he speaks from his own resources, for he is a liar and the father of it.

He is also a thief who comes to kill, steal and destroy.

That is why Jesus said in **John 10:10:**

The thief does not come except to steal, and to kill, and to destroy. I have come that they may have life, and that they may have it more abundantly.

The enemy satan, is a deceiver of the whole world – that is why His word in Revelations 12:9 tells us:

So the great dragon was cast out, that serpent of old, called the devil and satan, who deceives the whole world; he was cast to the earth, and his angels were cast out with him.

In love we are warning every person, the gay and lesbian included – do not be deceived, there is a deceiver out there. Do not be lied to – there is a liar out there.

Come back to God, embrace Him, embrace His word, follow Jesus, know the truth and the truth will set you free. The enemy satan and his demons cannot and will not be able to withstand the power of the word of God correctly understood. It will prevail and you will be set free.

Countless others have been set free, below are a few testimonies of individuals who were set free from homosexuality, by repenting and turning to Jesus Christ (1-3). It is important that people be given the choice to experience the love of Jesus Christ, to turn to God and be set free.

References:

Rosaria Champagne Butterfield – *The Secret Thoughts Of An Unlikely Convert – An English Professor's Journey Into Christian Faith.* Crown and Covenant Publications. ISBN 978-1-884527-80-7

Charlene Hong Afat Angela – *The Hidden Treasure Has been Found – My Story Delivered From Homosexuality.* Amazon Printers. ISBN 979-848-7996831

Joshua Hawkins Jr – *Delivered from Homosexuality, Freedom.* Amazon Printers. ISBN 9798610927480.

Chapter 10

Reflections From Other Church Leaders.

Through generations, God has delivered messages to his people through his prophets, pointing out the errors or the flaws in their lives and warning them to repent of their disobedience or face judgement. One is reminded of the story of Jonah, whom God commanded to travel to the great city of Nineveh to preach repentance to its inhabitants because of their wickedness. In his mercy, God sent his servant so that the people of Nineveh would not be judged of their wickedness. Likewise, the book Gay Marriage – what does Almighty God say? is a warning that God is sending a message through Apostle Max Matonhodze, to the leaders of the United Kingdom, particularly the Prime Minister and those who are responsible of passing laws in relation to the Same Sex Marriage Act. In short, this act crossed a line from heaven. Like the people of Nineveh, God, in his mercy and loving kindness, is telling the nation to repent the abomination of celebrating same sex marriage or face judgement. The people of Nineveh heard Jonah's message and repented. We pray that the leaders of the nation of the UK will hear Apostle Max Matonodze's message and get right with God.

CHURCH ELDER, BIRMINGHAM,
UNITED KINGDOM

Dear Apostle Dr Max

Thank you for asking me to preview this manuscript. My thoughts are as follows:

This book touches on the key area of the Same Sex Marriage Act of 2013. This Act ventures into an area of human existence that had remained sacred as laid out by God our creator. An unacceptable line has been crossed by the government when this said Act was endorsed and became law.

From a Christian perspective based on the Word of God, the Act is clearly not from God and is not for the benefit of the subjects of the UK nation, God's people.

The book walks you through the scriptures making it unquestionably clear that God's word directs against what this Act endorses. The source of the outline is clearly revelational and clearly from God Himself.

As a Christian nation with God's word as its foundation, the UK leaders are reminded of the responsibilities they have to direct the people along godly lines, according to His word and instructions. This book therefore is undoubtably a timely reminder, even warning to our leader the Prime Minister, of the inevitable consequences should heed not be taken.

Pastor Loxley English
London, United Kingdom.

Dear Apostle Dr Max

I congratulate you on this work and may the Lord use it as a source of change in this Nation. Please find my thought below as requested.

Let me first of all appreciate your courage to tread on this delicate terrain with the wisdom of God.

There is nothing more rewarding than obeying the voice of our Lord Jesus Christ no matter how difficult the command is. This is an important issue affecting our society and most importantly affecting our faith.

I have read through this book, and I agree with you about the love of God for all humanity in which the gay communities are not excluded. There have been many people who have come out of the gay community to tell their stories of how they were misled into becoming gay or lesbian, they were made to see the deceit in their gay status and sought God's forgiveness and reconciliation with their Maker. With all my heart, I love the LGBT community even though I disagree with their choices as a Christian because their choices are against the teaching of the Bible.

I believe if the government of this nation could repeal the said Act, it will save our nation from the wrath of God and do our young ones more good than evil. It is my prayer that God will bless this Nation and give the leaders a listening heart to do the right thing. The word of God in Proverbs 13:34 says *"Righteousness exalts a nation: but sin is a reproach to any people"*.

NHS HOSPITAL CHAPLIN
WEST MIDLANDS, UNITED KINGDOM

Dear Dr Max

As I said, the message in this book is revealing and to the point. Unfortunately, the Church seems to be sleepwalking into an abyss.

There appears to be a perception that being a Christian means you hate homosexuals. This is absolutely contrary to the word of God. God demands that we love our 'neighbours' but we don't have to agree with their perception.

I have friends who are homosexuals, and some are Lesbians. They are very much aware of my belief, but I care about them, and I let them know that I care about them.

That is what God demands of us.

May the Lord continue to bless you and encompass you as you serve Him diligently in His vineyard.

May the Peace of God be with you, in Jesus mighty name, Amen.

CHURCH ELDER AND NHS MEDICAL CONSULTANT
BIRMINGHAM, UNITED KINGDOM

After reading the manuscript, what I see is that God Almighty uses Apostle Dr Max to communicate His word to the top leadership of this nation and Apostle Dr Max gathered courage to communicate God's word on Same Sex Marriage Act.

Apostle Dr Max's manuscript points out that the one who is behind same sex marriage is satan and demons who plant in a person feeling towards a person of the same sex which is against the will of God.

The government's role is to promote righteousness but by legislating same sex marriage it means the government is helping satan to carry out his agenda openly. Almighty God wishes to bring to His people blessing, glory and bliss. The agenda of the enemy satan, is to steal, kill and destroy and bring shame into the lives of people. In the process satan seeks to frustrate the purpose of God in the lives of people.

Apostle Dr Max is urging the church not to just to sit and watch but to intercede for amelioration of judgement.

I would recommend this book to church leaders so that they have in-depth understanding of what God is saying.

The intention of this book should not be misunderstood, it is not to condemn the gay person but to reveal God's love and expose the tactics of the enemy satan.

CHURCH PASTOR AND ELDER
STAFFORDSHIRE, UNITED KINGDOM

Dear Apostle Dr Max

Thank you for asking me to preview the manuscript of Gay Marriage, what does Almighty God Say?. Yes, God loves gay and desires that they know Him and have a personal experience of His love, His mercy and His kindness. People can be completely delivered from gay spirits. They need to repent and seek help. A few years ago, I was ministering, and the Lord showed me a woman in the congregation who had come to church to seek help. I was shown in the spirit that while she was a woman there was upon her a spirit of a man. I called her to the front and prayed for her. After the service I spoke to her, and she confessed to me that she was lesbian. I counselled her on repentance and following Jesus. Over the coming months she was totally delivered, and she is now married with two children. Her lesbian partner also got delivered and is now also married. They both had come to church to seek help, they were willing to repent, receive counselling and to follow Jesus. We know that God is not a respecter of persons and the experience of these two can happen to anyone who repents and seeks to follow Jesus Christ. We give all glory to God.

Minister Clara
West Midlands, United Kingdom

Chapter 11

Reflections Of Apostle Bishop Cephas Nyemba

GAY MARRIAGE, WHAT DOES ALMIGHTY GOD SAY?

The word of God declares that God loved the world, that he gave it his only begotten son Jesus, so that who so ever believes in Him should not perish but have everlasting life *(John 3:16)*.

God's love is available to all. It is a universal provision for every sin including the gay life to be blotted away for all that will turn to God. All sinners are in a state of condemnation as the bible says "The wages of sin is death..." *(Rom 6:23)*. That includes gays and all sinners alike if they will not receive the love of God, repent, and begin to live a new way of life. For those who say, "God loves Gay", God's love of gay people is not based on or directed at the exclusivity of the gay lifestyle. God's love is universal to all.

This book gives the modern man, who is European, American, Russian, Middle Eastern, Asian, Australian, & African etc., a convincing declaration that God speaks to man today.

Its message speaks to this new age generation that is drifting away from its creator. God chose Apostle Max Matonhodze knowing that he will not buckle at the challenging task of conveying such a critical message that is also controversial. God knew he was going to obey resulting in the deliverance and salvation of many.

The source of the message of this book is God Almighty. He is the God who introduced Himself to His creation in the Bible saying, "I am the Lord your God (133 times) and "I am your God" (150 times). He is the creator of all things living and none living and the maker of man. Dr Matonhodze makes the existence of God who is the beginner of all things very clear. God, who has all authority, has established the way we must conduct ourselves as human beings, and we must obey. His word about man to man, and woman to woman lifestyle is very clear, He condemns it. But instead of judgement and destruction, God provided a way of salvation.

God who is King of Kings and Lord of Lords has chosen to channel His message through a nation that is a Kingdom. The United Kingdom is one of the many nations that has legislated laws to normalize the gay lifestyle. It is now the one used by God through Apostle Matonhodze as the messenger to communicate this empowered word to the nations. Now this word from God and written by Apostle Matonhodze must carry its authoritative, kingdom authority, and life changing power to every King, President, Prime Minister, and every Head of State. Nations must spread this message to their people, who must obey the word of God.

To obey God is key. This book provides a way for those who decide to allow Jesus to deliver their lives from a gay lifestyle. Life decisions are an activity of human will. As a function of the Holy Spirit of God, decisions are transformational.

Deciding to turn away from a life of bondage and submitting to Jesus one must use declarations like those listed below. This will help one to gain victory over strong negative feelings and thoughts and help take back control of one's life.

You are now saying:
I now know the truth of the word of God.
I reject the evil satanic influences that ensnared my life.
I chose to obey Almighty God who is God of all creation.
I denounce the gay lifestyle.
I denounce all sin. I ask God and His Holy Spirit to fill my life and help me to overcome the power of satan. I ask the Holy Spirit of God to help me to live a victorious Christian lifestyle.

That is, it. Praying earnestly like this moves God to answer your prayer and to change your life.

GAY MARRIAGE, WHAT DOES ALMIGHTY GOD SAY?

This book is simple to read and is easy to search for specific information that may be of interest to the reader. It is a great resource for anyone who seeks to understand the subject being discussed, and I highly recommend it to anyone who is seeking to know the truth, to be delivered and to share with others. God has spoken in this book. The nations must heed His word and be blessed.

APOSTLE BISHOP CEPHAS NYEMBA
PENNSYLVANIA – USA

Chapter 12

Conclusion

I have set out in this book a message which I received from Almighty God to give the Prime Minister of the United Kingdom and other world leaders. The capacity in which I write this book is as a Prophet and an Apostle (Special Messenger) of Jesus Christ, the King of Kings and Lord of Lords, by the grace of Almighty God, I have asked Church Leaders, who hear from God to read this message as independent witnesses and answer the question – do you believe this is the voice of God? They concur this message is the voice of Almighty God given in love for both the gay people and the nation of the United Kingdom and nations of the world.

Almighty God wants every gay person to understand that He loves them and wants each and every one of them to repent and receive His forgiveness and the gift of eternal life and live in His presence now and for all eternity. He wants the streets of the United Kingdom to be filled with His presence and be protected from judgement.

For Almighty God to speak in this manner is extra-ordinary which gives an imperative to the Prime Minister and other world leaders to act.

God is love. *(1 John 4:8)*. The embodiment of the love of God is in Jesus Christ, who came to seek and save those who are lost. He died for the sin of the world. The way to salvation in Jesus Christ is through repentance and repentance only.

Jesus Christ is overwhelmingly full of grace, loving kindness, and mercy. He is also full of truth, which is the correct understanding of the word of God.

The enemy of God and mankind, satan is a deceiver, the deceiver of the whole world, *(Revelations 12:9)* and a liar, and the father of lying. *(John 8:44)*. He is also described as a murderer, a thief, and a destroyer. *(John 10:10, John 8:44)*. His aim is to frustrate the purpose and plan of Almighty God for every man, woman, young man, young woman, boy and girl. God Almighty desires everybody to experience His love, culminating in experiencing His loving kindness, peace, joy and His glory, leading to an experience of life in His presence on the earth and eternal life in heaven.

The enemy satan, who has already been judged, *(John 16:11)* knows that he has a one-way ticket to the Lake of Fire for all eternity. His mission is to influence people through deception and lying, so that they live a life of shame on the earth and end up joining him in the Lake of Fire for all eternity.

We learn in the scriptures that it is appointed unto men once to die and after that comes the judgement. *(Hebrews 9:27)*. The scriptures also reveal that the judge will be Jesus Christ. *(Romans 14:10, 2 Corinthians 5:10)*.

God declares in His word "I am the Lord and I do not change." *(Malachi 3:6)* Jesus Christ is the same today, yesterday and forever. *(Hebrews 13:8)*. Heaven and earth shall pass away, but the word of God will not pass away. *(Luke 21:33, Mark 13:31)*.

We are living at a time when truth is often distorted, often many people think their feelings are the truth. Feelings can be manipulated by satan, and often human feelings change over time.

This book is written to send a message sent from Almighty God to the Prime Minister of the United Kingdom and to every other world leader, to:

a) Warn them as to the source of gay feelings, that they do not originate from God but are a result of deception and lies of the enemy satan. They are sown by satan.

b) Instruct everybody of the duty of love to people who are gay – this means kindness as demonstrated in equal opportunity in livelihood, education, employment, and free participation in society.

c) This also includes allowing them space and acknowledging their civil arrangements as depicted in the Civil Partnership Act.

d) Marriage is between one man and one woman only, is an institution ordained by God Almighty for allowing the expression of love between a man and a woman, consummated in a physical union between a man and a woman which results in bearing children and the promulgation of humanity. As such it is an integral institution for the multiplication of humanity. God has honoured this institution as sacred to Him and from beginning of creation, He made a man and a woman as complementary to each other to make a whole family unit. The relationship between a man and a woman in marriage is also a mirror image of the relationship between Jesus Christ and the church.

e) The Same sex marriage act must be repealed.

i) Celebrating same sex marriage moves the gay further into enticement by the enemy satan, deeper into embracing deception and lies of the satan and therefore further from repentance.

ii) Same Sex Marriage Act causes reproach from heaven to any nation. This is because righteousness exalts a nation, but sin is a reproach to any people. *(Proverbs 14:34)*. Reproach means disapproval, disappointment, rebuke, and disgrace. This means when there is righteousness there is grace and when there is reproach there is judgement. Righteousness is conducive with the presence and the working of God in a nation but sin which is co-operating with the enemy satan, results in judgement because of the absence of the protection of God. Sin drives out the presence and working of God and results in the working of the enemy satan in a nation.

iii) In the same token children should not be raised up by same sex couples because this environment is not the will of God for children to be raised. Children were meant by Almighty God to be raised in an environment that demonstrates to children the complementarity of a man and a woman working together to raise a family.

For the good of both the gay people and our nation we ask the Prime Minister to seek audience with His Majesty to discuss the contents of this book. This is imperative as Almighty God has spoken and to Him, we give all the glory.

About the Author

Max Matonhodze is an Apostle and a Prophet, medical practitioner, and author who, in his own words, "has a message to Planet Earth from Almighty God." As the Founder and General Overseer of Planet Ministries, Dr Max serves the people of Planet Ministries church and the world at large, and he has a message of hope and glad tidings for the hurting, the guilty, the lonely, and the discouraged.

This book Gay Marriage – What Does Almighty God Say? – is his second book following an extra-ordinary visitation by Almighty God on Monday the 6th January 2014, with a message for the Prime Minister of the United Kingdom as well as other world leaders. It is therefore written in a Prophetic capacity in that he is a messenger of Almighty God to the Prime Minister and other world leaders, to the nation and other nations of the world.

It reveals the mind of God on same sex marriage with extra-ordinary clarity.

It is written for anyone, irrespective of nationality, language, or tribe and irrespective of whether you were brought up as a Sikh, Hindu, Muslim, Protestant, Catholic, Buddhist, Jain or Communist. Or whether you consider yourself Atheist, Agnostic or anything else.

If you are sincerely asking the questions-

What are the origins of gay feelings?
What does it mean to say God is love?
How do I access the love of God?
Does God love gay people the same as everybody else?

This book answers these questions with extra-ordinary clarity.

It reveals the truth of the word of God sent to set people free.

It uncovers the deception which the enemy of God and mankind satan, has used to keep God's people under bondage.

His word says – **"And you shall know the truth and the truth shall set you free"** *(John 8:32)*.

The truth is the word of God correctly understood.

To be set free from the bondage and deception of the enemy satan, you need to understand the word of God correctly.

This book is written to give you insight into the truth, which is eternal, which does not change with fashion or time.

This book is written to expose the deception of the enemy satan by which he wants to entice the people of God.

His word also says – **"Sanctify them by Your truth, Your word is truth"** *(John 17:17).*

To sanctify is to set yourself apart for God, to do that you need to understand where enemy lines are. You need to understand where God is and where the enemy is, what God says and what deception the enemy is enticing you into.

It is only after sanctifying yourself for God that you can experience His grace and His power.

By His grace and His power anyone can be set free, to experience the love of God and to experience eternal life.

His word says in John 17:3 **"And this is eternal life, that they may know You, the only true God, and Jesus Christ whom You have sent."**

Eternal life is the experience of God and Jesus Christ, it begins right here on the earth and into all eternity. God wants you to experience Him, His grace and His power and that will only begin after the word of God has been understood correctly, enemy positions have been identified correctly and you have made up your mind to repent which is changing your mind to align with God's position and committing yourself to Jesus Christ who died and shed blood for the redemption of mankind.

This book is written to give you an experience of the love of the God of Jesus Christ and to set you completely free from the bondage of the enemy satan and usher you into a life of service to Almighty God of Jesus Christ.

Dr Max Matonhodze is a qualified Respiratory and General Internal Medicine Specialist. His medical qualifications include Bachelor of Medicine and Bachelor of Surgery (Mb ChB) from University of Zimbabwe, Master's Degree in Medicine from University of Zimbabwe, Member of the Royal College of Physicians of Ireland (MRCPI), Certificate of Completion of Specialist Training (CCST-UK) from the Joint Royal Colleges of Physicians Training Board of the United Kingdom (JRCPTB). He is Fellow of the Royal College of Physicians of London (FRCP) and holds a Master of Arts in Medical Education (M A Med Ed) from Keel University.

After medical qualification worked in the health service in Zimbabwe for 9 years before coming to England in December 1993. After working in various training grades, was appointed Consultant Physician in General and Respiratory Medicine for Walsall Healthcare NHS Trust on the 10th of June 2002, a post he has held for 21 years.

Having been brought up Catholic including spending six years in a Catholic boarding school (Gokomere High School in Masvingo, Zimbabwe) he had personal experience of the love of Jesus Christ while an undergraduate medical student in August 1980 when he became a born-again Christian. Following this he felt God was calling him to become a preacher of the gospel.

Almighty God subsequently revealed to him that his calling was in the capacity of an Apostle. What followed were dramatic experiences with Almighty God. Notable among these experiences is that on the 30th of November 1987, the Lord Jesus Christ appeared in his bedroom in visual form and commissioned him to send God's Message to Planet Earth.

Planet Ministries was launched on the 18th of May 2012 following another encounter with Almighty God that night. On the 11th of August 2015, He was instructed by God to send out the Planet Daily, a daily devotional message. This has been sent as a daily blog from the Planet Ministries website

https://planetministries.org.uk

as well as on social media and WhatsApp groups. At the time of writing of this book, he has sent out more than two thousand daily blogs over the last seven years.

This book is the second book by Apostle Dr Max Matonhodze. His first book *Vessels of Excellence* is a result of 40 years of an experience with Almighty God of Jesus Christ and teaching which has been delivered over the same period.

Helping you to become the best you can be.
You may be asking:
Is there God?
Is it possible to know Him intimately?
How can I become a better person?
How can I overcome some of the human weaknesses I have?
I have lost my way - any way back? *Yes there is!*

If you are looking to produce the best **YOU** there can be... read on. This book will help you become a *Vessel Of Excellence.*

www.ingramcontent.com/pod-product-compliance
Lightning Source LLC
Chambersburg PA
CBHW032011080426
42735CB00007B/568